WHAT AR

HAVE YOUR CAKE AND . . .

In 1941, Mrs. A.A. Vial baked 150 cakes to be distributed at random among the soldiers in Europe. One young man bit into his cake and discovered a wedding ring; he realized that it belonged to his mother—Mrs. Vial.

LUCKY NUMBER?

One day in 1958, a Jersey Central railroad train plummeted from a bridge into Newark Bay. A photographer captured the shot of the rear car being lifted from the water by a crane. Clearly visible on its side was the number 932. The next day thousands of New Yorkers put their money on 932 in the local numbers game. The bookies took a big loss when the number came up.

FORE! . . . ORDAINED . . .

Michael Scaglione became so incensed after missing a golf shot on the thirteenth hole, he threw his club in disgust at his golf cart. The club shattered and part of it rebounded, stabbing Scaglione and killing him instantly.

CHARLES BERLITZ'S WORLD OF THE INCREDIBLE BUT TRUE

CHARLES BERLITZ

FAWCETT CREST • NEW YORK

A Fawcett Crest Book
Published by Ballantine Books
Copyright © 1991 by Charles Berlitz and the Stonesong Press, Inc.

ISBN 0-449-22012-5

Printed in Canada

First Edition: January 1992

CONTENTS

FOREWORD

The realm of the odd and the awesome where human eyes cannot see and our intelligence becomes insignificant is all around us. It abounds with mysteries. Mysteries of unusual appearances, mysteries of phenomenal strength or odd creatures constantly remind us that we do not truly know all that we suppose. What, for example, happened to Judge Crater, Amelia Earhart, or Jimmy Hoffa? Did Napoleon actually end his life on St. Helena or, as some surmise, did he live out his life in New Orleans? Will the theory of a second Kennedy assassin ever be verified? But these examples are personal mysteries that can be (and perhaps already have been) solved.

Greater mysteries include the disappearances of cities, cultures, great islands, and entire civilizations, like those of the Maya, the Toltecs, the Indus Valley, the islands of the Pacific, and the peoples who preceded the Incas in South America. Many of these early civilizations achieved remarkably accurate concepts of the world and the universe, well in advance and in different parts of the world from civilizations that followed them, often attaining scientific expertise not to be equaled again for thousands of years. Such impossibly advanced civilizations have burst into flower and then disappeared or regressed, for reasons unknown, either into more primitive jungle and desert tribes or have been absorbed by other, less advanced populations.

Despite our own advanced state of technology, we are frequently visited by mysterious "ghosts"—and not just the kind that haunt our houses but more modern ghosts such as those of radio and television shows of years past suddenly appearing and disappearing on channels showing regularly scheduled programs. Do such unexplainable events point to the possibility that there exists a curvature in space or time? More and more reliable witnesses are reporting such events which are said to occur by day as well as by night. So many reports can't be ignored. They have become the object of study by scientists as have numerous cases of possession or poltergeist activities, the latter being violent out-of-body projection of one's own personality or "soul." It has even been suggested that the increasing number of sightings of UFOs, now firmly believed in by more than 50 percent of the world's population, may be the modern equivalent of ghosts at a time when haunted houses are being replaced by haunted skies.

The greatest mysteries of the world do not consist of incidents, however fascinating, but of the potential solution to elusive questions pertaining to the nature of time and space. Space, with its suns, planets, and denizens (if any), has long been the object of intensive study, and it is likely that within a very few years the surface of Mars will be explored by expeditions from earth to learn, among other things, whether what appear to be gigantic pyramids and an enormous stone human face in a section of Mars now called Cydonia are really what they seem to be and whether they have been constructed not by nature but by living entities. Also scheduled to be examined on Mars are the apparent ruins of a seaport city on the shores of a now dry ocean bed. These and other ruins have been photographed by American and Russian astronauts and, if verified as true constructions, regardless of being hundreds of thousands of years old, their existence should provide the comforting thought to the peoples of the earth that we are not alone in the universe. (Unless, of course, the constructions were built by our own ancestors before they came to earth!)

As we penetrate further into the exploration of space and time we will be opening up new worlds of wonder, changing our own consciousness and destiny. This, again, is the kingdom where our imagination will be as important as our intelligence.

Consider what the famous French scientist Marcellin Berthelot wrote in 1887 regarding the progress of science and the exploration of space:

> From now on there is no mystery about the universe . . .

If he had had the capability of listening, he and others might have heard in response to their insular surety echoes of cosmic laughter from somewhere beyond space and time.

DOUBLE COINCIDENCE TIMES THREE

One of the oddest coincidences ever recorded spans a period of nearly a hundred years and involves three ships that sank off the coast of Wales in the Menai Strait. The first vessel went down on December 5, 1664, and of its eighty-one passengers only one, Hugh Williams, survived. On December 5, 1785, 121 years later, another ship sank in the Menai Strait and, again, all of the passengers perished except one—named Hugh Williams.

Two ships sinking in the same area on the same day of the month certainly isn't earth-shattering. When each of them has only one survivor and both are named Hugh Williams, it's a little eerie. But the story doesn't end at that.

On December 5, 1860, yet another ship, a small, twenty-five-passenger vessel, sank in the Menai Strait. And once again there was only one survivor—and once again his name was Hugh Williams.

COPTIC VISION

In the suburbs of Cairo, Egypt, a glowing apparition has been seen over the roofs of two Coptic churches, mystifying believers and skeptics alike since April 1968. Appearing in the early morning hours and described by some as resembling the Virgin Mary, the vision first appeared over St. Mary's Coptic Church in Zeitûn. For three years, thousands of people flocked to the sight to witness the nightly phenomenon.

After its last occurrence in 1971, the apparition didn't appear again until 1986, when the figure rematerialized atop St. Demiana's, another coptic church outside Cairo. According to eyewitnesses, the vision was often accompanied by the scent of incense and the entire dome of the church would glow while the image hovered over it.

The crowds grew so large outside St. Demiana's that the Cairo police went in to keep order. Mousad Sadik, a reporter who regularly covered the story for a Cairo-based newspaper, told of one occasion when the spirit was visible for a full twenty minutes. While scientists have attempted to credit fraud, mass hallucination, a natural optical phenomenon, or electrical discharges from the roof of the church, no one has definitively explained the phenomenon.

ELECTRO-OSMOSIS

Joe Orchard, a former petty officer of the Royal Navy, and his family began experiencing strange phenomena in their Adisham, Kent, home in the mid-seventies. Doors and water faucets would inexplicably detach and fly around. A ceiling collapsed for no apparent reason, furniture would mysteriously become soaking wet, and electrical appliances regularly malfunctioned. Circumstances finally convinced the Orchards to flee their home.

After some consideration, Orchard concluded that "electro-osmosis" was causing the disturbances in his home. A power cable near the cottage, he presumed, was leaking electricity which was subsequently affecting the mechanics of the house. The Orchards moved back in only after burying electrodes in the lawn to deflect the leaking power.

They then took legal action against the South Eastern Electricity Board, seeking restitution for the damage done to their home. The utility denied responsibility, however, and enlisted a sympathetic judge to discount the Orchards' claims. After a twelve-day trial, the judge declared that Joe, his wife, June, and their twenty-three-year-old son had staged the whole ordeal to bilk the electric company. "We told the truth in court, but we were branded liars," June stated afterward.

TRANSPOSING SENSES

It's generally believed that when people lose the ability to see or hear, their other senses somehow compensate for the deficiency and become noticeably more acute. But in several documented cases, the lost sense has actually been shown to relocate.

The most celebrated case of transposed senses was reported by Dr. C. Lombroso, a highly regarded neurologist and psychiatrist. Three months after a fourteen-year-old girl had suddenly become quite ill, she completely lost her sight. Even though her eyes were nonfunctional, however, the girl claimed she could see. Her mystified parents took her to Lombroso who conducted a series of tests to determine if she was telling the truth.

The neurologist placed blindfolds over the girl's eyes and

then placed objects in front of her. Amazingly, she could, in fact, see them, identifying colors and even reading a letter. A bright light shone against her earlobe, however, caused her to wince in pain. And when the doctor poked his finger at the tip of the girl's nose, she angrily exclaimed, "Are you trying to blind me?"

Evidently the girl's sense of vision had relocated to the tip of her nose as well as to her earlobe. But more than her sight had been transposed: apparently she could also smell through her chin.

RETURN FROM SUICIDE

On November 8, 1952, Theresa Butler took an overdose of sleeping pills and was found hours later in her bathtub. She was taken to the morgue after she was pronounced dead by the local coroner who found no pulse, no blood pressure, and no perceptible reflexes.

The morgue attendant on duty was accustomed to seeing an occasional bout of rigor mortis, a condition that can cause a dead body to suddenly move reflexively. He wasn't prepared, however, to see Butler's corpse working its jaw and gasping. Stunned, and not a little frightened, he called his boss who determined that Butler wasn't dead after all and immediately rushed the now comatose woman to the hospital.

It's not often that someone recovers after being declared legally dead. But that's exactly what Butler did, and five days later she was discharged from the hospital. Fortunately, her condition had been discovered before she was buried alive.

PSYCHIC SEA SEARCH

In 1977, the Mobius Society, a parapsychology research group based in Los Angeles, set out to test the ability of psychics to predict the locations of sunken ships. Director Stephan Schwartz sent sets of four Pacific Ocean navigation charts to five volunteers, all of whom claimed to have some psychic ability but did not practice professionally. They were asked to locate and describe the shipwreck site through nothing more than remote viewing, using a mental image to sense an actual ship.

In what was already a great coincidence, four of the five participants selected a single site: ten square miles near the island of Santa Catalina. According to the four psychics, a wooden sailing ship with a steam engine had exploded sometime between eighty-two and ninety-three years earlier. They also described such objects as the ship's wheel and a stone slab that would be found at the site, located some 277 feet below the surface.

That June, Schwartz and two of the psychics set out to determine the accuracy of the prediction. Also aboard the ship was Al Witcombe, who would pilot the *Taurus I,* a thirty-two-foot submarine. After three hours of fruitless searching, Witcombe dropped a radio homing device into the target zone. *Taurus*'s manipulator arm dug into the sand on the ocean floor and pulled out the first of many relics from the sunken ship located by the homing device.

Three days of diving proved incredibly successful. Every object the psychics had envisioned in the remote viewing experiment was found, including the wheel and the stone slab. The distribution and type of wreckage, moreover, supported the psychics' claim that the sunken ship was made of wood and had, indeed, exploded. And the marine growth on the wreckage indicated that the ship had been underwater for decades.

THE MANY LIVES OF THE DALAI LAMA

To practitioners of the centuries-old religion of Tibetan Buddhism, the epitome of spiritual leadership and perfection is the man-god known as the Dalai Lama. His significance stems from the Buddhist tenets regarding reincarnation.

To Buddhists, the ultimate goal of reincarnation is nirvana, at which level all the karmic requirements of human life have been satisfied and the soul may rest in its enlightened state. More advanced souls, however, may choose to remain in the cycle of reincarnation in order to help others on their own paths toward nirvana. Among such beings, called *bodhisattvas*, the most sacred is Avalokitesvara, the Bodhisattva of Compassion. Each Dalai Lama, throughout the history of Buddhism, has been believed to be the reincarnation of Avalokitesvara.

Upon the death of each Dalai Lama, the monks consult oracles to determine within which child the spirit of the Avalokitesvara has been reincarnated. Once found, the child is tested to verify the spirit's presence and to determine if the child will be the new Dalai Lama. The ritual requires the child to correctly select his predecessor's possessions among a miscellaneous collection of objects. This is possible because, unlike mere mortals, bodhisattvas retain their memories of past lives.

Many other stories surround the Dalai Lama. For example, when the Chinese Red Army had solidified its control over China in 1950, the Chinese Communists reestablished Chinese sovereignty over Tibet, signing a treaty with the Dalai Lama in 1950. The Tibetans, however, continued to resist but were finally overcome in 1959. A prize of the Chinese victory would have been the capture of the Dalai Lama, the spiritual head of millions of Tibetans and Chinese. But the Chinese never captured him, although he was accompanied by numerous escorts which the special Chinese troops using advanced aircraft should have found easily.

As the Dalai Lama approached a mountain pass leading to freedom in India, a heavy and unexpected fog suddenly covered the border area making it impossible for planes to locate him, and a convenient blizzard obscured the traces of his passage from the pursuing troops.

He established himself in India, where he still is, fortified by his claim to the stewardship of Tibet, and protected, evidently, by the Tibetan gods of snow and fog.

THE LOST FLEET OF
ALEXANDER THE GREAT

In 234 B.C., Alexander the Great, after extending his conquests as far as western India, ordered Admiral Nearchus to return to the Persian Gulf and transport the exhausted and depleted Greek troops back to Greece. Some of the naval fleet, however, never reached their homeland. Some historians speculate that their ships continued past India into the Pacific Ocean, eventually reaching Tahiti and Hawaii. There has been some evidence to support the idea that the Greeks even made it all the way to the western coast of the Americas.

On the east coast of North America, the first white men to reach the shores of Maryland and Virginia discovered a river the natives had named Potomac. Similarly, the Greek word for river is, oddly enough, *potamós*.

When sixteenth-century Spanish conquistadors invaded the Aztec empire, for example, they learned that the word for the Aztec pyramid temples was *teocalli*, meaning "dwelling of the god." Later study by historians revealed that *teocalli* is remarkably similar to two Greek words— *theós* and *kalías*—which, when used together, also mean the same thing as *teocalli*.

And in Hawaii, a number of words such as *aeto* (eagle), *mele* (song,) and *noo-noo* (intelligence,) are strikingly close to Greek words with the same meaning—*aetós, melodía*, and *nous*. Hawaiian war helmets, moreover, although designed in wood and feathers instead of metal and horsehair, were nearly identical to their Greek counterparts.

The simple but intriguing explanation for the appearance of Greek language and artifacts in far-flung cultures centers around Alexander, conqueror of most of the ancient world. After overpowering the mighty Persian Empire, Alexander's land troops pushed eastward into India and northward into what is now the Soviet Union. Meanwhile, his eight-hundred-vessel fleet, led by Admiral Nearchus, explored the Indian coast.

If the Greeks did find their way to lands in the South Pacific and the Americas, they would probably have seemed like demi-gods, and their language and art worthy of adoption into native cultures.

TALKING PORPOISES

Some years ago, a shipment of recently captured porpoises was placed in a holding pool at the Miami Seaquarium. The pool was located near another one containing tamed porpoises, but it was out of sight. The intention was to train the new porpoises so that they, too, could entertain the Seaquarium audiences. The lessons, however, would not begin until the following day.

During the night, J. Manson Valentine, curator honoris of the Museum of Science of Miami, heard a barrage of sounds emanating from both porpoise tanks. In the morning, when it came time to begin teaching the new additions, Valentine and his training team discovered that the lessons weren't necessary: the new porpoises were able to perform most of the tasks on the first try.

Valentine surmised that through some form of inter-porpoise communication, the veteran porpoises had informed the new ones what would be expected of them.

HAUNTING AT HAW BRANCH

Haw Branch Plantation had once been a magnificent estate, with gardens, rolling lawns, dry moat, and stately chimneys gracing the classic antebellum manor house. But in 1964, after fifty years of neglect, the property had fallen into grave disrepair. When Gibson McConnaughey inherited Haw Branch, she and her husband, Carey, immediately set about restoring the estate to its former grandeur. There was at least one ancestor who would also return to Haw Branch.

Soon, however, the McConnaugheys began hearing strange noises throughout the house. Sometimes the scent of oranges or roses would waft through the air, even when neither the fruit nor flower was present. On one occasion, moreover, the husband and wife saw someone carrying a lantern as he came out of the barn and approached the house, but as he drew near they could see only the kerosene lamp bobbing in the air.

Three months after they had moved into Haw Branch, the couple and their children were awakened in the middle of the night by a woman screaming in the attic. Petrified, they waited until morning to investigate, but found nothing to account for the noise. The screams continued to recur at six-month intervals, but it wasn't until the summer of 1967 that Gibson witnessed an image connected to the voice.

"She was not transparent, just a white silhouette," Gibson later recalled. Although she was unable to discern any facial features, Gibson noticed that the apparition wore a floor-length dress from some earlier era. Standing only briefly in front of Gibson, the woman stared silently into the distance as she repeatedly disappeared and then reappeared.

By 1969, the family had grown accustomed to the woman and their other ghostly housemates. The biannual visit of the woman's voice, however, began to occur more frequently after the arrival of a family heirloom. Gibson's elderly cousin sent the McConnaugheys the portrait of a long-dead relative named Florence Wright. From the description they received, the family expected a portrait in vivid pastel colors depicting Florence in her younger days, shortly before her sudden death. When it arrived, however, the McConnaugheys were surprised that the painting was awash in dark grays, browns, and dirty whites. Even so, they hung it over the library fireplace.

Then, in February 1970, the portrait began a transformation. The charcoal black hair seemed to be a lighter shade. A rose at the base of the painting was turning from dusky gray to pink. And Florence's skin was taking on a lifelike hue. In fact, every detail was inexplicably bright and more colorful. As the process continued, the image of Florence Wright soon depicted a blue-eyed, red-haired beauty sitting in a bright green chair.

According to a psychic who subsequently examined the portrait, Florence's spirit had been locked in the painting at the time of her death. She therefore had the power to drain the artwork of all color until she was happy with its location. The voices heard at Haw Branch were fellow spirits who had been enlisted to aid the woman in regaining her lost color. Evidently, the psychic believed, Haw Branch, with its vibrant spiritual atmosphere, was a satisfactory home for Florence Wright.

UFOs over Japan

Some seven hundred years before the term *flying saucer* appeared in Western accounts of UFO sightings, the Japanese were recording incidents of their own. Ancient documents, for example, describe an unusual object heading north from a mountain in Kii province on the equivalent in Western dating of October 27, 1180. The craft then simply disappeared over the horizon, leaving a luminous trail in its wake. In another instance, a poet's execution was stayed in 1271 when an object suddenly appeared in the sky on the day of the scheduled beheading.

It was also a Japanese military officer who ordered the

first known UFO investigation in 1235. On the night of September 24, General Yoritsume and his army witnessed mysterious lights that remained visible in the sky for many hours, swooping, circling, and performing other then unimaginable aerial maneuvers. The general's experts, however, finally reported that the phenomenon was the result of "the wind making the stars sway."

Indian Observatory

In Arizona, Saskatchewan, and some fifty other sites throughout North America, there are distinct wheel designs laid out on the ground but discernible only from above. The wheels are simply constructed out of thin ridges of stones making up a rim, hub, and often a number of spokes. Some wheels also feature piles of stones called cairns strategically placed within the wheel's outline. The Bighorn Medicine Wheel is the best preserved and best known of the North American wheels. So named by the Plains Indians because of its supposed spiritual properties, the Bighorn Medicine Wheel is located high on a plateau in Wyoming's Bighorn Mountains.

Historians suspect that the wheels, like their European counterparts, the megaliths, were astronomical observatories used by local tribes as early as the 1100s. A particular cairn of the Bighorn faces the wheel's hub and directly toward the rising sun of the summer solstice. Other rock piles point toward the rising and setting of three brilliant stars during seasonal changes. All the wheels, moreover, were evidently designed to afford a clear view of the horizon.

But while historians are reasonably sure of the wheels' mechanics, they are still puzzled by their purpose. Some researchers speculate that the medicine wheels would be especially helpful to agricultural tribes in keeping track of the planting seasons. Nomadic hunting tribes could also use them to observe the roaming bisons' migratory patterns, or perhaps their own migration to warmer climates during the winter.

DEATH OF THE OCEANS

Oceanographer and conservationist Jacques Cousteau proposes a horrifying vision of the consequences of mankind's present exploitation and pollution of the world's oceans.

If all the oceans' aquatic life were to suddenly die, decaying organic matter would produce an unbearably foul stench. The wafting odor would drive people from the fertile coastlines and into the mountains and highlands that could barely support the overwhelming influx of new inhabitants.

Far worse, however, would be the release of carbon dioxide into the atmosphere. Left to its own devices without aquatic life to aid in balancing the earth's salts and gases, the gas would steadily increase, creating a greenhouse effect. Rather than the earth's heat radiating into space, it would be trapped beneath the stratosphere, raising sea-level temperatures to intolerable degrees. Polar ice caps would melt, creating flooding of unimaginable proportions.

As nightmarish as such prospects may seem, they aren't the only likely possibilities. As the thick film of dead organic matter coats land and sea, the slime would interfere with evaporation and subsequent rainfall. The result would be global drought and famine.

The ultimate consequence, thirty to fifty years after the oceans officially die, would be the extinction of the human race. Confined to overcrowded areas between dead seas and sterile mountains, and suffering from starvation, disease epidemics, and severe weather, humans will finally succumb to anoxia, or lack of oxygen. And then life on earth will be reduced to bacteria and a few remaining species of insects.

If this eventuality is likely to come to pass, and the process may have already started with the poisoning of oceans and seas, now would be a good time to begin the study of space lifts to other planets, hopefully those with a good supply of water.

NAZCA PATTERNS

Pilots flying over southern Peru's Nazca desert in 1939 unexpectedly observed strange patterns on the ground. Depictions of animals and birds as well as spiral and straight lines, they claimed, resembled the runways of modern airports. Even more amazing, the designs' measurements were incredibly accurate. Some fifty years later, scientists are still unable to explain the origins of the massive drawings. Because the designs are discernible only from the air, however, many researchers speculate that their ancient creators also must have been able to fly—or were directed by someone else who could.

To space buffs like Swiss author Erich von Däniken, the

designs' explanation is simple. The Nazca drawings, he believes, are signal markers for aircraft guidance and were placed in the Peruvian desert by extraterrestrial visitors. In his 1967 book *Chariots of the Gods?*, von Däniken proposed that the alien beings arrived on Earth about ten thousand years ago and proceeded to manipulate monkey genes to develop a species of humans. Their creations would then perceive the aliens as gods.

Biblical and other creation stories, von Däniken suggests, stem from those early extraterrestrial visits. Archaeological findings like Nazca are the relics of ancient astronauts.

THE MYSTERIOUS MAYAN CALENDAR

Devised more than five thousand years ago, the ancient Maya calendar is amazingly accurate. Its computerlike complexity baffles archaeologists and astronomers: among their other feats, the Mayans correctly determined that the sun, moon, and the planet Venus appear in the same alignment only once every 104 years. Of all ancient races the Maya came the nearest to reckoning the exact length of the solar year. Our present reckoning is 365.2422 days, while the Maya, using their own calculations and instruments from their high pyramids, came to 365.2420, a difference of .0002 of a day, thousands of years before anyone else came near it.

How were the ancient Mayans able to make precise astronomical observations long before the invention of the telescope? According to the civilization's own legends, the calendar was a gift of "strangers from the star world."

GROUP REINCARNATION

In 1962, English psychiatrist Arthur Guirdham began treating a young woman experiencing terrifying nightmares. During the next four years, "Mrs. Smith" (as Guirdham called her in three books about the curious case) recounted torments she endured as a member of the Cathars, a thirteenth-century French religious sect whose followers staunchly believed in reincarnation.

The historical details and portrayals of thirteenth-century life in Smith's accounts were amazingly accurate, Guirdham found. Smith claimed, for example, that the Cathars' robes were dark blue, contradicting most historians who had always indicated that the garments were black. Digging into reams of research and data, Guirdham was finally able to determine that Smith was right.

Smith was only the first of several reincarnated Cathars that Guirdham began to attract. Eventually six others joined her, forming a closely knit group. And having sensed something familiar about Smith's tales from the very beginning of their association, Guirdham also began believing he was the reincarnated Roger Isarn de Fanjeaux, Smith's lover during her thirteenth-century incarnation. It would certainly explain why the others had found the psychiatrist.

PSYCHIC WITNESS

When a seven-year-old boy disappeared from his Los Angeles home in 1978, police were stymied in their efforts to find substantial leads in the case. In frustration, they turned to a local psychic known simply as Joan.

Joan soon told the detectives that the boy had been murdered by a man she described to a police artist. She later disputed the accuracy of the sketch, insisting that the face should have been longer and the nose smaller. The missing boy's father, however, was still able to identify the depicted suspect as a family acquaintance, and he was subsequently arrested.

At the beginning of the trial, the defense attorney argued for the dismissal of charges against the acquaintance. Based solely on psychic predictions, the suspect's arrest had been illegal, the lawyer stated. Even so, the judge overruled the courtroom objection and the acquaintance was eventually convicted of murder.

THE CASKET LID OF PACAL

A carving found in Palenque, Mexico, on the casket cover of a Mayan nobleman proved to be a surviving treasure of Mayan pictorial art. It was excavated in a crypt beneath a pyramid temple and is assumed to be the casket and portrait of someone named Pacal. Archaeologists have offered the theory that Pacal was a former Mayan ruler, although it is difficult to ascertain much about him since the Mayan system of writing, a series of hundreds of complicated glyphs, has not yet been satisfactorily deciphered. Regardless of his name, however, he must have been a person of supreme importance to have been so entombed.

It is not certain what the coffin lid represents. When the rectangular lid is viewed on its long side, it looks like a feathered and jeweled Mayan figure riding or straddling some sort of stylized form, thought by some archaeologists to be the Tree of Life. In addition, there seems to be some sort of monster depicted on the lower part of the lid.

Another theory, held by certain Russian space engineers, scientists, and writers such as Aleksandr Kazentsev, suggests that the picture is a stylized rendition of an astronaut or cosmonaut. Kazentsev has pointed out that many of the unique details in the carving evoke the peculiar control panel of a capsule designed for space travel. When the carving is placed horizontally, the seated position of the astronaut appears correct for a space probe. Kazentsev has pointed out details of a recognizable antenna, space directional system, control panel, turbo compressor, and, behind the picture of Pascal, items that resemble fuel tanks and a turbine and combustion chamber.

While it is evident that here, as with many mysterious archaeological finds, what you see in the carving depends on the way you look at it, it can't be denied that the coffin lid of Pacal represents at the very least an extraordinary coincidence.

Out-of-Body Experiences

Intentional and random out-of-body experiences (OBEs) have been reported throughout history by people of every age, race, creed, and culture. OBEs are as common among Russians and Americans, say, as they are in the primitive tribes of Africa and Australia.

Writers and artists especially claim that OBEs serve as creative inspiration and they have been able to describe them in vivid detail. Famous out-of-body travelers include D. H. Lawrence, Aldous Huxley, Emily Brontë, Jack London, and the German poet Geothe.

During World War I, American author Ernest Hemingway served in the United States ambulance corps. One hot July night in 1918, he was crouched in a cramped trench on the Italian front near the village of Fossato when he suddenly heard a mortar shell hurtling through the air. The bomb exploded and shrapnel seared his legs. Afterward, he told friends that the pain was excruciating and he had believed he was near death when he actually felt his spirit leave his body.

Hemingway immortalized his experience in the 1929 novel *A Farewell to Arms*. "I tried to breathe, but my breath would not come," says the protagonist Frederic Henry. "I felt myself rush bodily out of myself and out and out and out and all the time bodily in the wind. I went out swiftly, all of myself, and I knew I was dead and that it had been a mistake to think you just died. Then I floated, and instead of going on I felt myself slide back. I breathed and I was back."

A GLIMPSE OF HEAVEN

Father Filippo de' Neri was considered an extraordinary holy man in sixteenth-century Rome. Parishioners had observed him levitating during Mass, performing exorcisms, and even raising the dead.

At dawn on March 16, 1589, Neri was summoned to the palace of Italy's Prince Fabrizio Massimo. The priest was told that the prince's fourteen-year-old son, Paolo, was gravely ill and not expected to live much longer. Even though the boy died half an hour before Neri arrived at his bedside, the priest knelt to pray for the departed soul, blessing the body with holy water.

As the grieving family looked on, the holy man blew into Paolo's face, placed a hand on the youth's forehead, and called out his name. In a moment, Paolo's eyelids miraculously flickered and opened.

Paolo told the people gathered around his bed that he had gone to heaven and had seen his mother who had passed away eight years earlier. Heaven was a beautiful place, the exalted child said, and he desperately wanted to return. "Well, then," the priest told him, "go in peace and be blessed." With that, Paolo closed his eyes and died—again.

THE SHARKS IN THE FOREST

Scuba divers who encounter sharks in clear water generally believe that sharks, unless aroused to a feeding frenzy by another source, will not attack them on sight. The divers, with their bulky tanks, safety equipment, and clouds of bubbles seem to give sharks the instinctive feeling that they represent an opponent who requires further reconnoitering prior to attacking. In other words, people are in greater danger swimming on the surface, kicking their legs like a wounded or dying fish, an easy prey to a shark, than a diver cruising slowly through the deep water like a fellow predator.

Unusual exceptions to this rule, however, have been reported in the Pacific area south of San Francisco, where sharks have taken to attacking and killing divers for food in the underwater kelp forests off the coast. The kelp rises from the ocean floor like trees with branches and leaves. This not only makes it harder for divers to distinguish hungry sharks but also seems to convince the sharks that the divers, which they might not ordinarily attack, are really seals, a local shark delicacy. Divers may resemble seals to them because of their glistening diving suits, fins, and even their method of propulsion, as they swim through the tree-like kelp formations off the coast of northern California.

LIFELINES OF THE
NOT-QUITE-DEAD

Among the medical community in nineteenth-century Europe and America, the establishment of death was often a difficult task. Bodies were often interred as quickly as possible to avoid contagion, particularly during cholera and typhoid epidemics. And in the absence of modern embalming techniques, it was not uncommon for people to be buried when, in fact, they weren't really dead. In Germany alone, it was estimated that thousands of premature funerals occurred every year.

Children's fairy tale writer Hans Christian Andersen and others wrote about the possibility of waking to find themselves buried alive. Andersen, moreover, never went to bed without leaving a note on his nightstand. It read: "Am merely in suspended animation." And a few days before he died, Andersen instructed a friend to open the writer's veins following the event to guarantee that he was no longer living when buried.

This common fear of being buried alive created a burgeoning market for various safeguards. One of the most basic was a setup that included a bell placed at ground level, its wires running into the coffin. In this way, a person who revived after burial could ring the bell to alert the living. More advanced versions featured a pneumatically operated signaling device triggered by the slightest movement inside the casket.

Perhaps the most elaborate death guard, however, was a Viennese mechanized morgue, planned in 1874. Corpses would be monitored by metal plates that could detect body movement and then send an electrical impulse to trigger an alarm in the central control room. An identification number on each bell would enable watchmen to determine which body had moved so they could rescue the person.

The morgue plans, however, were abandoned when a new cemetery, complete with the popular aboveground bell system, was laid out nearby. There are no indications in the cemetery records that any of the presumed dead ever rang the bells.

KEEPER OF THE PSYCHIC WOLVES

When Jack Lynch took over the wildlife reintroduction project to save the American buffalo wolf from extinction, he didn't expect his wards to display an uncanny psychic ability. The animals, however, seemed to have developed intense ties to their savior, E. H. McCleery, who had established the sanctuary. Lynch, familiar with wolf behavior, took over the job as caretaker when McCleery, suffering with colon cancer, became too ill to continue tending his beloved wolves.

On the night of May 23, 1962, Lynch was surprised by the animals' howling in unison. "If they are disturbed by something, they might howl for about twenty seconds," Lynch explained. "But this time, they kept it up for ten minutes."

The next day, Lynch learned that McCleery had died at the exact time the wolves had begun howling. "I have no explanation for it," Lynch said, "especially since [Mc-Cleery] was in a hospital thirty-six miles away. I just know what I saw and heard."

DREAM OF THE CAVE DWELLERS

Anthropologist Joseph Mandemant once reported a prophetic dream in which he found himself in the famed Bedeilhac Cave. In the French cavern, prehistoric hunters gathered around a fire. On the ceiling, Mandemant could clearly see hunting scenes obviously painted by the cave's occupants.

Mandemant was struck by the presence of a man and a woman, who he presumed were lovers. They left the main area and disappeared through a short cleft and into a smaller, more private space and onto an outcropped ledge. As the anthropologist watched the two humans huddle in the darkness, a sudden loud roar erupted as the ceiling of the cave collapsed, sealing the room where the couple had been.

When he awakened, Mandemant recorded every detail of the dream and then set out for Bedeilhac Cave. At first, he seriously thought the trip was a wild-goose chase. Inside the cave, however, he located a huge slab of limestone in the spot that seemed to be the same location as the cleft leading to the lovers' private space in his dream. He tapped on it in various spots and heard an encouraging hollow sound. He hired workmen to break through the stone and, sure enough, on the other side found the lovers' space and the ledge.

While there was no trace of the prehistoric lovers, Mandemant did find the crude but elaborate hunting scenes he had first seen in his dream.

THE HUMAN BLOWTORCH

At first, it might have seemed entertaining, but A. W. Underwood grew tired of his ability to set objects aflame by simply breathing on them. It was, after all, a talent he had to carefully guard. And despite months of tests, and the eventual celebrity status he achieved, not one expert could explain what caused the bizarre phenomenon.

According to L. C. Woodman, the first physician to examine the fire starter, when Underwood took such items as a cotton handkerchief and dry leaves and held them against his mouth, they would burst into flames in a matter of seconds. The doctor rinsed the twenty-four-year-old man's mouth out with various solutions. He made him wear rubber gloves. No matter how rigorous the examination, neither Woodman nor his colleagues could find any trace of trickery. Nor could they determine any medical reason that would cause such symptoms.

ROGER WILLIAMS'S APPLES

Roger Williams was one of the most honored and beloved of the New World's early settlers. Having first arrived in Massachusetts from Cambridge, England, in 1631, he was later banished to Rhode Island for his outspoken religious views. In his new home, however, Williams became the leader of the tiny colony, famed for its unprecedented religious freedom.

When Williams died in 1683, he was buried in a grave marked by a modest headstone. Some years afterward, however, Rhode Island officials decided to erect a more appropriate memorial. When the grave was opened, to everyone's amazement, it was empty.

At first, the Roger Williams memorial commission members suspected grave robbers had stolen the leader's remains. But, in fact, it was nothing so sinister. It seems that as the roots of a nearby apple tree had grown, they pushed their way into the coffin where they overtook and eventually absorbed the remains of Roger Williams. The evidence was the tangle of roots that bore a remarkable resemblance to a human body.

The commission decided to remove and preserve the roots which are now in the possession of the Rhode Island Historical Society.

THE FORMER LIFE OF SHANTI DEVI

Born in 1926 in Delhi, India, Shanti Devi was only three years old when she began talking about people she referred to as her husband and children. Questioned by her mystified parents, Shanti said the spouse's name was Kedarnath. Both he and a son, moreover, lived in Muttra.

Thinking the girl was suffering from some sort of delusion, her parents took her to a doctor. While there, Shanti recounted even more details of her other life, including her pregnancy. She had died during childbirth in 1925, she told the physician.

By the time she was eight years old, Shanti had been examined by half a dozen doctors, but no one had gone beyond questioning the girl. Her granduncle, however, finally decided to investigate her story and tracked down the man Shanti said was her husband. Kedarnath did, indeed, still live in Muttra with his two children, the youngest having been the child his wife had died delivering in 1925. But believing he was being tricked, Kedarnath declined to meet the girl himself and sent a cousin to Delhi in his place.

When the cousin arrived at the Devi home on the pretext of conducting business with Shanti's father, the girl immediately recognized him. After discussing and agreeing on many details of the deceased woman's life, the cousin was convinced of Shanti's recollections and he sent for Kedarnath.

Some time later, Shanti finally went to Muttra to meet her former family, but they wanted nothing to do with her, and Shanti would have to learn to live in the present. By this time, however, the case had garnered the attention of the press as well as past-life researchers. Many of them thoroughly investigated her claims before Shanti could begin the process of adapting to her new life. The case remains one of the best documentations of past-life recall in history.

THE GARRULOUS
GLASTONBURY MONKS

During his research of Glastonbury Abbey in 1907, prior to its eventual excavation, Frederick Bligh-Bond was frustrated in his attempts to locate the former sites of two particular chapels mentioned in many early descriptions. Since all other alternatives had failed, the British architect and archaeologist considered the use of automatic writing to enlist the aid of the spiritual world.

One of the most famous historical sites in England, Glastonbury Abbey is said to have existed during the lifetime of Jesus Christ. According to legend, Christ himself had visited the religious enclave. Kings, including, many believe, Arthur, had been buried in its chapel. By 1086, it had become a shrine and the objective of pilgrimages. During the reign of Henry VIII, however, the abbey was destroyed, a consequence of the king's battles with the Catholic Church. Eventually, the remains of the massive structure crumbled until finally nothing remained of the former magnificence.

Although Bligh-Bond initially planned nothing more than an experiment in automatic writing to locate the chapels, he called upon a friend, a certain Captain Bartlett, proficient in producing written messages from otherworldly entitles. Amazingly, the "spirits" were sympathetic to Bligh-Bond's plight. Soon they began spouting incredibly detailed information about the location and measurements of the abbey's chapels. The communicators, moreover, identified themselves as former Glastonbury occupants, mostly monks. At least one, however, had lived there some thousand years before construction of the actual abbey and described the support for the roof of a hut he had designed and that was later uncovered by Bligh-Bond's workmen. Each communicator responded to particular questions relating to his own tenure at the abbey.

Using the information furnished by the spirits, Bligh-Bond surveyed the area around the former site of the abbey. Subsequent excavations proved all the details to be correct, often accurate to within a fraction of an inch. Authorities had no doubt that the Glastonbury discoveries were legitimate. When Bligh-Bond revealed how he located them, however, he lost a great deal of credibility. Although the excavation continued, Bligh-Bond was driven off the project in 1922. Ten years later, in his book *The Gate of Rememberance,* he not only wrote about the messages he had received and verified by the excavation but also revealed other descriptions of the abbey which were also later confirmed.

VELIKOVSKY, THE BIBLE, AND THE PLANETS

Immanuel Velikovsky, a Russian-born author who came to America in 1939, provoked a scientific storm eleven years later with his book *Worlds in Collision,* the echoes of which are still reverberating in the world of science. Based on his studies of ancient history, Velikovsky attempted to show that the stories from the first books of the Bible, so often considered legends, were basically historical and were corroborated by the legends of other ancient races existing at the same time.

Velikovsky claimed that the earth had indeed experienced planet-shaking catastrophes as "recently" as two thousand years ago during which periods, as recorded in the Bible, the sun had stood still in the heavens, the Red Sea had parted and joined again, manna had fallen from the skies and sustained the Israelites, great plagues had beset Egypt—in short, that the miracles of the age of Moses were factual. He maintained his theories by even more surprising suppositions: that part of the planet Jupiter had torn off and formed a comet; that the comet had swerved near Mars, knocking Mars off its orbit to a near collision with earth, and that the comet had continued its path within our own solar system periodically causing tidal waves and enormous earthquakes on earth until the comet became the planet Venus.

According to Velikovsky human mass destruction has been detailed in almost all ancient records, and mass animal extinctions are evidenced by remains in caves and strata throughout the world. Despite Velikovsky's assiduously compiled corroboratory evidence from ancient writings and legends, his theories were generally ridiculed by the scientific establishment. A distinguished British astronomer stated that his book was "all lies," adding that he "had not read and would never read (it)." Another astronomer said it was "the worst book since the invention of movable characters." The public, as might be assumed, read it with enthusiasm.

This author asked Velikovsky shortly before his death how he had been able to predict, long before it was "officially" known, that the surface of Mars was covered with craters, that Venus spins in a contrary direction to other planets in our system, and that the planets and sun have positive and negative electrical charges. He also asked how he knew in advance that the temperature of Venus would be plus eight hundred degrees Fahrenheit when Einstein himself had predicted that it would be minus twenty-five degrees Fahrenheit?

Velikovsky answered in a somewhat indirect manner. He

said: "You know the British Museum has thousands and thousands of Babylonian baked clay tablets which have not yet been translated or published. They offer interesting and pertinent information about the solar system to anyone who takes the trouble to read them." It should be added that Dr. Velikovsky had great expertise in the languages of the ancient Middle East and was able to read the inscribed cuneiform texts of Assyria and Babylonia.

THE ANCIENTS KNEW ABOUT ANTARCTICA

In 1513, Piri Ibn Haji Memmed, an officer in the Turkish navy who was known as Piri Re'is, had cartographers prepare a map of the Atlantic Ocean and its bordering lands. Afterward, it was forgotten until 1929 when it was found in the Turkish imperial archives in Constantinople. Drawn just twenty-one years after Columbus discovered America, it was one of the most accurate early maps of the New World. An inscription on the map indicated that Piri Re'is based the western portion on maps that Columbus himself had used during his first voyage. It was the first evidence that there had been earlier maps and supported the idea held by many researchers that Columbus had known about and used them. Another inscription, moreover, stated that the Turkish officer had also consulted even older maps, some dating to the time of Alexander the Great.

The map also presented proof that the unexplored Antarctic continent had been mapped by someone thousands of years before it was rediscovered in 1820. It shows, in correct proportion, parts of Africa and eastern South America. Beneath the southern tip of South America, there are contours of another coastline. Cartographer and historian Charles Hapgood has identified these as the coastline and mountains of Antarctica as they actually exist under the covering ice sheet. What is more unbelievable for an ancient map is that it was drawn using spherical trigonometry and adapted to the curving of the earth, thousands of years before it was possible to figure longitude.

As it is known that Antarctica was largely ice free about 8000 to 10,000 B.C., a number of explanations for the advanced mapping have been offered, including the theory that this was an air map made by extraterrestrials from a UFO.

Charles Hapgood disputes the UFO theory as follows:

It is . . . reasonable to suppose that the land was occupied and that the occupants could make maps. I feel that only commercial motivation could have led to the mapping: somebody wanted the natural resources and the trade of the continent.

It is unrealistic to jump to the conclusion that . . . extraterrestrials made the maps. The maps in their present state do not suggest the accuracy we should attribute to people capable of crossing billions of miles of interstellar space . . .

With the mention of commercial motivations Hapgood may have explained the survival of the Greek or proto-Greek maps of an earlier world. They were preserved by constant copying by shipmasters who wished to keep secret the trade routes to far places. The Oronteus Finaeus map, last copied in 1532 from an ancient original, shows rivers flowing through Antarctica which follow the path of present glaciers. Still another, the Buache world map, dated 1754, shows Antarctica at the bottom of the world and explains that the undiscovered land must exist to balance the land areas. But the then unknown continent was drawn correctly—with one notable exception: it was shown as two enormous islands, separated by a sea, which is actually the true shape of Antarctica without the ice.

The existence of Antarctica was finally accepted as a reality in 1820. But it was not until the Geophysical Year of 1955 that an international scientific expedition verified that the true coast of Antarctica is obscured by the ice; that there are mountains and riverbeds under a two-mile-high ice cover, and that the continent itself consists of two islands.

One mystery remains. What was the advanced civilization whose representatives charted the far area of the globe when the world was much younger and Antarctica had not yet been frozen over?

UFOs over Africa

Zimbabwe air force officials are still baffled by a round, shiny unidentified object with a cone-shaped top that swooped over the southern part of their African nation in 1985. According to Zimbabwe's Air Commodore David Thorne, air traffic controllers watched the craft hover overhead and even tracked it on radar. Pursuing the UFO, air force pilots got a good look at it as the craft streaked the sky. They described it as being so shiny that at first it seemed to reflect the colors of the sunset, but as the sky grew darker, however, they realized that the UFO was creating its own light. The pilots also estimated that the UFO was traveling at twice the speed of sound. "Our pilots are completely reliable," Thorne insisted. "This cannot be dismissed as a plane, weather balloon, or natural phenomenon."

Celestial Swastika

The swastika, in modern times, has become a symbol of evil, but according to two University of Texas scientists, the Nazi emblem may have mystical connotations. When physicists C. J. Ransom and Hans Schluter exposed hydrogen gas to electricity and magnetism, the hydrogen glowed. Then the gas suddenly parted to form the silhouette of a swastika. The experiment led the scientists to speculate that a comet, passing through the earth's magnetic field, might create a similar effect. If so, then the swastika would have first appeared to humans as a naturally occurring phenomenon, but awestruck observers would have taken it as a supernatural sign. That, they concluded, would explain why the modern symbol of evil was once revered by the Hindu and other religions. Swastikas are carved, for example, on ancient tombs near the city of Troy. And even Christians portrayed it as a holy symbol during the Middle Ages.

Roman UFOs

In his manuscript *Prodigerium liber,* fourth-century Roman historian Julius Obsequins recorded numerous accounts of UFO sightings. In one particular incident, a round, shiplike shield with flaming torches gyrated and fell to the ground near Spoletium, north of Rome. "It then seemed to increase, rose from the earth, and ascended into the sky, where it obscured the disk of the sun with its brilliance," he wrote.

Obsequins's reports, however, were not the only ones to be recorded and survive into the twentieth century. In *Prodigerium ac Ostentorium Chronicon*, a professor of grammar and dialetics compiled other Roman sightings whose descriptions are remarkably similar to modern accounts of UFOs seen flying in formation. During the reign of Emperor Theodosius I, for example, in the last years of the fourth century a glowing orb suddenly appeared in the sky, shining almost as brightly as Venus. As witnesses gazed in awe, a great number of other similar objects amassed, like a swarm of bees flying around a beekeeper. They seemed, moreover, to be dashing violently against each other, and eventually joined to form a shape resembling a two-edged sword.

THE IMAGE IN THE
CHALLENGER SMOKE

When the U.S. space shuttle *Challenger* exploded on January 28, 1986, a nation watched in horror as the lives of seven American astronauts and heroes, including one teacher, ended tragically. That night, one witness repeatedly watched a videotape of the disaster hoping, perhaps, to grasp its reality. Viewing the tape closely, however, she noticed an image that greatly affected many devastated employees at the Kennedy Space Center.

Now a Kennedy Space Center medic, Debi Hall witnessed the disaster firsthand, seated alongside reporters and the astronauts' families. At home, exhausted and emotionally drained by the day's events, Hall initially thought she was imagining things when she sat in front of the television. She kept rewinding the tape and playing the scene back until she convinced herself that, yes, there was an image of Christ in the clouds of smoke enveloping the *Challenger*.

The following day, she and her husband viewed the tape together and he agreed that there was clearly an image of a large, bearded face. And when Hall took the videotape to the space center, others also saw the face, without it being pointed out to them. Hall's explanation? "I think it shows divine intervention," she says.

CAPTIVE EXTRATERRESTRIALS

During the summer of 1983, Larry Bryant of Alexandria, Virginia, served a writ of habeas corpus on the United States Departments of Defense and State, the Air Force, the Army, the National Security Agency, and the Federal Bureau of Investigation (FBI). His charge? All the defendants had conspired to cover up the 1947 crash of an extraterrestrial vehicle in the New Mexico desert. What's more, the Air Force actually possessed one or more bodies of the UFO's occupants.

An FBI document appended to the court order quoted an Air Force investigator as saying three flying saucers had been recovered near the Pentagon's huge radar apparatus in New Mexico. Evidently the radar had interfered with the craft's controlling mechanism. According to the memo, each circular craft had a diameter of approximately fifty feet and contained a raised section in the center. Their occupants were humanoid, it continued, three feet tall and wearing metallic bodysuits.

Bryant believed the extraterrestrial visitors were still alive and being held against their constitutional rights. They could not be held without being charged with a crime, he argued, and by serving the writ Bryant hoped to have the aliens released by the government or, at least, to recover their bodies. Perhaps he wished mostly to make the affair public; it's not likely that the government, after years of UFO denials, was going to now acknowledge the existence of UFOs, let alone the possession of aliens themselves, because of a simple item such as a writ of habeas corpus.

THE BERMUDA TRIANGLE REVISITED

An area bounded by an imaginary line stretching from Florida to Bermuda to Puerto Rico and then back to Florida, the Bermuda Triangle has been the site of many mysterious disappearances of boats, planes, and people. One of the oddest incidents occurred during a short flight to Grand Turk Island in the Bahamas.

As Helen Cascio piloted her Cessna 172 and approached the island, the control tower imparted her landing instructions. But Cascio didn't respond, although her radio channel was open. The tower operators heard the pilot telling her lone passenger, "I must have made a wrong turn. That should be Turk, but there's nothing down there. No airport. No houses. Nothing."

The controllers continued frantically to attempt contacting the pilot, but Cascio obviously could not hear them. Then they received what would be the final query they would hear: "Is there no way out of this?" No trace of the plane, pilot, or passenger was ever found.

Explanations of many investigators for the bizarre disappearances in the Triangle range from hijackings by modern pirates to simple human error. There is also some speculation that the area is located over a whirlpool or a hole in the ocean that swallows vessels and aircraft unfortunate enough to pass directly overhead.

Another possibility, however, is that parts of Atlantis lie beneath the Bermuda Triangle. Fabled Atlantean pyramids, constructed as power sources, may still sporadically function and disrupt vessels' and aircrafts' communication and control systems.

Then, of course, those who believe we are being invaded by malevolent or devious extraterrestrials speculate that these aliens can somehow lock into the Bermuda Triangle's magnetic field and extricate human specimens and artifacts for their own research purposes.

While many disappearances in the Bermuda Triangle have been widely reported, however, less has been heard about craft appearing in the area. In July 1975, for example, Jim Thorne, a member of an oceanic research group aboard the yacht *New Freedom*, photographed a dazzling electrical storm above the Triangle. Examining the developed film, he was shocked to see a clear image of a square-rigged boat an estimated hundred miles from the *New Freedom*. Yet on the night of the storm, he knew there had been no other vessels in the vicinity.

THE MYSTERIOUS MARTIAN CANALS

When Italian astronomer Giovanni Schiaparelli discovered a grid of lines on the surface of Mars in 1877, he theorized that the canals, as he called them, had been created by inhabitants of the red planet as some kind of irrigation system to conserve their dwindling water supply. Later, some observers thought the lines might, instead, be trails followed by herds of migratory Martian animals.

Many others, particularly today, suggest the so-called canals were actually dried-up riverbeds. There are, in fact, strong indications that there is still surface ice at the planet's poles. But until spacefarers are able to physically explore the planet, the explanation for the Martian canals will remain a mystery.

THE UNKNOWN PLANET

Every schoolchild is taught that there are nine planets in our solar system. But for more than a hundred years, some astronomers have postulated that there may, in fact, be a tenth.

The scientific speculation began in March 1859 when a French country doctor and amateur sky watcher named Levearbault observed an object orbiting the sun. It seemed to be even closer to the sun than Mercury, considered by most astronomers to be the closest planet orbiting the sun. Levearbault meticulously tracked and timed the assumed planet's path, recording his observations on a pine board.

When France's most illustrious astronomer, Urbain Jean Leverrier studied Levearbault's records, he agreed that there was, indeed, another planet, which he subsequently dubbed Vulcan. According to Leverrier, Vulcan's presence would explain why Mercury moves forty-three inches closer to the sun every year. Vulcan's gravity, he proposed, was actually pulling Mercury toward it.

Even so, no one since has observed Vulcan—perhaps because many don't believe the planet exists and are, therefore, not looking for it. Yet some of these same skeptical astronomers have speculated that a tenth planet, which they have likewise never seen, does exist, but in the other direction, beyond Pluto.

THE CITY THAT VANISHED TWICE

There are a number of legendary lost cities on the bottom of the Atlantic Ocean and the Mediterranean, Aegean, and Caribbean seas. There are also a number that are certainly drowned but not lost, as their locations are known. The ancient Roman seaside resort of Baiae, for example, is not far from Naples and has been explored and extensively photographed by divers working at a depth of fifty to sixty feet. Sybaris, whose name has become synonymous with luxurious or "sybaritic" living, lies on the seafloor of the Gulf of Taranto. Parts of Carthage, Leptis Magna, Tyre, Caesarea, Alexandria, and other large cities still lie under the waters of the Mediterranean.

Such cities have usually subsided into the sea as a result of seismic action and are easily located because the ancient chroniclers told us where they were. Something unusual, however, happened to Helike, a large city of classical Greece which in 373 B.C. disappeared from the surface during an earthquake and tidal wave with all of its buildings, streets, ships, and thousands of inhabitants. No one escaped the final towering wave which swept away not only the ships of Helike but also ten visiting warships from the Spartan fleet anchored in the harbor. Where Helike used to be there were only the waters of the Gulf of Corinth.

When the waters cleared it was possible to see the ruins of the city on the seafloor. For hundreds of years, Helike stayed in its undersea location, perfectly visible through the clear water. Roman tourists of a later epoch would contract Greek boatmen to row them over the well-preserved ruins. The tourists would often employ divers to bring up coins and other finds from the undersea city. The divers plunged up to fifty or sixty feet through water with crystal-clear visibility. From the surface, a statue of Zeus (Jupiter to the Romans) could be seen still standing amid the ruins of his temple.

Toward the end of the Roman occupation of Greece, however, another earthquake opened the seafloor under this underwater Pompeii and then closed over it. Helike, now lost, may have contained treasures of considerably greater value than the silver and gold coins the divers were seeking.

Unless a new shock brings the city again to the surface, Helike may lie where it is forever, both lost and not lost several miles east of the present town of Aíyion on the northern shore and an unknown distance beneath the seafloor of the Gulf of Corinth.

THE PHARAOH AND THE ALIENS

An ancient Egyptian papyrus may contain one of the first known written accounts of a UFO sighting. According to the record, dating from the time of the Pharaoh Thutmose III, who reigned from about 1504 to about 1450 B.C., scribes in the House of Life sighted a "circle of fire" traveling silently through the sky. "It had no head," the papyrus states, "and the breath of its mouth had a foul odor." The awestruck observers fell to the ground, not knowing whether to fear or worship the strange celestial flame. During the next few days, more and more similar fireballs, as bright as the sun, appeared over Egypt.

In an effort to ward off the objects' power, the pharaoh directed the priests to burn incense to encourage the peaceful intercession of the gods. And when the unidentified objects finally departed, Thutmose ordered the written record so that the incident would always be remembered.

LIZARD MAN

There have been numerous Bigfoot sightings in the United States and around the world. The humanlike creatures are usually said to be large and hairy with glowing red eyes. During the summer of 1988, however, residents of

Bishopville, South Carolina, reported accounts of a rare breed of Bigfoot: a seven-foot-tall lizard man with green scaly skin. According to witnesses, unlike other Bigfoot creatures Lizard Man has only three toes on each foot, as well as long apelike arms that end in three fingers tipped with four-inch claws. Only the second Bigfoot to have only three fingers on each hand, and the first to also have three toes on each foot, Lizard Man is the most unusual Bigfoot ever reported.

Seventeen-year-old Chris Davis first encountered Lizard Man around 2:00 A.M. on June 29. On his way home, the teen stopped near the brackish waters of Scape Ore Swamp outside Bishopville to change a flat tire. While replacing the jack in the car's trunk, he glimpsed something running across the field toward him. Jumping into his 1976 Toyota Celica, he was quickly engaged in a tug-of-war with the reptilian creature as he tried to pull the door closed. Then Lizard Man jumped onto the car's roof, where he left scratches in the paint as evidence of his attack.

Hysterical, Davis returned home and told only his parents and a few close friends about the experience. Law enforcement officers, however, interrogated him after neighbors said the boy might know something about the strange bite marks and scratches found on another car.

Davis wasn't alone in his report. Soon other reports were flooding the sheriff's office. Teenagers Rodney Nolfc and Shane Stokes, for example, were driving near the swamp with their girlfriends when Lizard Man darted across the road in front of their car. Construction worker George Holloman also claimed Lizard Man jumped at him as he was collecting water from an artesian well.

Investigating the area around the swamp, state trooper Mike Hodge and Lee County deputy sheriff Wayne Atkinson found three crumbled, forty-gallon cardboard drums. The tops of saplings were ripped off eight feet above the ground. And there were, according to Hodge, "humongous footprints," fourteen-by-seven-inch impressions in hard red clay. Following the tracks for four hundred yards, the officers backtracked and found new prints impressed in their car's tire tracks. According to state wildlife biologists, the footprints matched no known animal species.

CITIES WITHOUT NAMES

The jungles and deserts of the earth contain a number of "lost" cities, lost because their impressive ruins leave little suggestion of what race built them, and why they were abandoned. Their locations, often in deserts, deep forests, or under the sea, bear witness to past cataclysms, man-made as well as natural. Time has covered them under a jungle canopy or buried them under great mounds of earth.

Most of the lost cities of Europe, the Middle East, and southern Asia can be linked to an identifiable culture. The ruins of Ankor Wat in Cambodia, the mound-covered cities of Babylonia, the sunken cities of the Mediterranean, and even the island ruins of the Pacific can be identified because of their similarities to other cultures. But what once were huge cities, like Mohenjo-daro and Harappa in Pakistan, have no cross references in ancient records. These large metropolises, which flourished thousands of years ago, once contained populations of over a million inhabitants. But no one knows their true names or what race built them. All available records are written in a hieroglyphic language which no one yet has been able to read. The only other place this language has appeared is on Easter Island, the Pacific island of colossal statues, almost exactly on the other side of the earth from Mohenjo-daro and Harappa.

Some of the prehistoric cities of South America are especially puzzling because their location atop tall mountains makes one wonder how enormous stones, weighing hundreds of tons, could possibly have been transported and set exactly in place. We do not know what these cities were originally called because they were already deserted when the Spanish explorer-conquerors arrived. The American peoples who greeted and later fought the Spanish had given the ruins different names and when questioned said that the cities had been built by the gods.

There is an intriguing legend of a lost city which is reported to still exist in the Amazon jungles. The city is reputed to contain great treasure, not buried but, in some versions, still in use by the inhabitants of the city. These survivors are said to preserve their isolation by being surrounded by bellicose Indian tribes notably unfriendly to explorers. The inhabitants of this lost city are said to be of a white race, and it is reported that they still possess an advanced culture and many accoutrements of civilization, including a means of illumination, not electric but a constant glowing light which is not fire.

Portuguese and other explorers have been trying to locate this mysterious city since the seventeenth century. An early expedition led by a Francisco Raposo ascended a precipice over the jungle and reached a plateau. They saw a large city about four miles away. When they approached the city they found it was apparently abandoned but only partially in ruins and that a number of large stone buildings were still standing. There were streets, plazas, walls, arches, and obelisks ornamented with what appeared to be writing. Statues, carvings, and the style of architecture were superior to those of other pre-conquest South American cities. Mine shafts outside the city indicated a high content of silver ore. While exploring, Raposo and his men saw some "white Indians" in a canoe dressed in strange garments. The expedition, fearing an unequal combat, quit the area. Other expeditions have unsuccessfully tried to retrace the route, and one of them, with hundreds of men, disappeared in the jungle.

Colonel Percy Fawcett, a retired British army officer, was undoubtedly the most dedicated among the explorers who continued the search. At different periods from 1906 to 1925 he searched for and compiled information about this lost city which he considered to be in the vicinity of the Xingú River, a tributary of the Amazon, in Brazil. He thought it was part of a whole civilization and that there were other cities also buried in the jungle. He believed, too, that the lost city was a remnant of an old advanced civilization, its people now degenerate, but one which still preserved the remnants of a forgotten past.

His dedication to his research ended in 1925 when he himself disappeared on his final expedition. The last entry in his diary, later found, indicated that he thought he was within a two-week trek of the city that he had so long tried to find.

Did he find it and decide to spend the rest of his life there? Or was he killed by the Indians he once said might be guarding it? The disappearance of Colonel Fawcett is one of the major mysteries of exploration. His own words would be a fitting epitaph: "What can be more enthralling than penetration into the secrets of the past and throwing light onto the history of civilization itself?"

THE PROPHECIES AT FÁTIMA

More than seventy years ago, three shepherd children claimed they saw the apparition of "a beautiful lady from heaven" who eventually entrusted them with three secrets. Although two were eventually disclosed, the third remains locked in a vault in the Vatican.

Lucia, Francisco, and Jacinta claimed to have seen the apparition in a cloud hovering over a tree near the village of

Fátima in Portugal. The mysterious woman told them to return to the same spot on the thirteenth of each month. On the appointed day, one month later, the children trekked back to the oak tree, followed by some fifty other villagers who had heard the children's tale spread throughout Fátima.

While some witnesses later claimed that there was, indeed, a low-hanging cloud over the tree, no one except the children saw the woman. The results were no different the following month, and soon skeptics were berating the children as well as the adults who had been taken in by the game. The children, however, insisted they were telling the truth.

Despite the seething of church officials, the children continued to return to the tree on the thirteenth of every month. On a rainy October 13, 1917, which would prove to be the last occurrence of the apparition, the site was mobbed by faithful Catholics desperately hoping to experience a miracle. Although the children were still the only ones to see her, the woman identified herself as "Our Lady of the Rosary" and divulged the three secrets. Then the vision vanished. Suddenly, villagers later reported, the rain stopped and the clouds dissipated, revealing a sun that seemed to begin spinning and plummeted to the ground. The terrified crowd was certain that the world was coming to an end, but the sun soon returned to its normal position. The bizarre behavior was said to occur twice more.

But what about the secrets kept by the children? They were never divulged by Francisco or Jacinta, who died during the influenza epidemic of 1918. Lucia, however, later wrote an account of the experience in which she described the predictions, at the request of the Holy See. One was a vision of hell, she wrote, and another concerned the outbreak of World War II.

At the lady's request, Lucia said, the third secret must never be divulged and, indeed, remained in a sealed envelope until Pope John XXIII opened it in 1960. The revelation so terrified His Holiness that he reportedly ordered it resealed and never made public.

A CURIOUS MEETING OF COMPATRIOTS

The now legendary sinking of the passenger ship *Andrea Doria* was a worldwide news event. But one of the lesser-known tales associated with the disaster involved a bizarre meeting of compatriots.

The *Andrea Doria* was destroyed when a Swedish ocean liner plowed into its side, penetrating the passenger cabins. In one of the cabins, a young Norwegian girl, alone and panic-stricken, began screaming in her native language.

It just so happened that one of the Swedish liner's crew, a Norwegian sailor, heard the girl's cries for help. They seemed to be right outside his own cabin. Pushing through the splintered wall of the ship, he was able to reach directly into the girl's cabin aboard the *Andrea Doria* and pull her into his cabin.

The ships had collided at the exact area where the two Scandinavians had their cabins.

THE METEOR AT FOREST HILL

The morning of December 8, 1847, was clear and sunny in Forest Hill, Arkansas. By the end of the day, people would be debating the cause of events that had transpired.

By midafternoon of that early winter's day, churning gray clouds had mysteriously accumulated, blotting out the sun and darkening the sky. The clouds seemed to be illuminated by "a red glare as of many torches," according to one eyewitness account. Suddenly, there was an ear-splitting explosion. Buildings shook and the church steeple's bell began ringing. Then, a barrel-sized object with a trail of flames hurtled from the sky.

The fiery ball struck the earth just outside Forest Hill, creating an indentation that measured more than two feet in diameter and eight feet deep. At the bottom of the hole, a huge rock steamed. It was, in fact, so hot that water poured into the hole instantly condensed to steam. The air, investigators also noticed, was pungent with the aroma of sulfur.

Some experts, of course, believe the hurtling ball from the sky was a meteor, even though meteors are not known to be accompanied by a sudden cloud formation. According to others, a flash storm produced lightning that struck the ground, fusing the soil into a type of rock called fulgurite. But this explanation doesn't account for the projectile that witnesses saw fall from the sky.

Starvation in the Palace

A plowboy in fifteenth-century Cheshire, England, Robert Nixon was a mentally retarded young man, generally quiet. Few people paid attention to his occasional outbursts of babbling verbiage. And it wasn't until he was called into the service of the king that anyone realized his talent.

One afternoon while working in the field, Nixon suddenly and inexplicably exclaimed, "Now, Dick! Now, Harry! Oh, ill done, Dick! Oh, well done, Harry! Harry has gained his day!" It meant nothing to his coworkers and normally they would have forgotten all about the incident. But the next day, a passing courier from London reported that King Richard III had died in combat against the forces commanded by the king's rival, Henry Tudor. The battle, the Cheshire folk learned, had occurred the previous day and, it seemed, at approximately the same time of Nixon's puzzling declaration.

When Henry Tudor, now Henry VII of England, heard about the incident, he sent for the retarded visionary, but Nixon became hysterical when the command was delivered. He was petrified of going to London and begged not to go. If he did, he said, he would surely starve to death. But despite his protestations, he was soon escorted to the palace where Henry intended to initially test Nixon's abilities.

As he had planned, Henry hid a valuable diamond, claimed that he had lost it, and asked Nixon to find it. Nixon, however, was more talented than the king presumed. He calmly and coherently said, quoting an old proverb, that anyone who hides an object should certainly be able to find it afterward. So there was no need, he told the king, to tell His Majesty, where the diamond was.

Henry was so impressed, it's said, that he installed Nixon in the palace to have the new palace prophet's predictions recorded. And during his royal employment, Nixon foresaw the English civil wars and the war with France as well as the deaths and abdications of kings. Only one of his prophesies—that the town of Nantwich will be destroyed during a great flood—has yet to come true.

Despite his successful tenure in the king's service, however, Nixon was continually plagued by the fear of his own starvation. To ease his prophet's mind, Henry ordered that Nixon be fed whenever and whatever he wanted, which did not endear Nixon to the kitchen staff. And when he was away from the castle, Henry also assigned an officer to watch over Nixon's welfare.

The officer, it seems, took his orders quite seriously, locking Nixon in a closet to protect him from any violence. Once, however, when he was suddenly called away from the palace during the king's absence, the fact of Nixon's being in the closet slipped the guard's mind. And by the time anyone found him, Nixon had starved to death.

PURE CHANCE

Frederick Chance was speeding down a lonely road in Stourbridge, Worchestershire, England, when he saw the headlights of an oncoming car. Both vehicles were traveling at such speeds that they were unable to swerve in time to avoid a collision. Emerging from the wreckage with only minor injuries, Chance checked in the other car and satisfied himself that its driver was also relatively unharmed. Thankful that the accident had not been worse, Chance introduced himself to the other driver. The motorist was incredulous, for he, too, was named Frederick Chance.

PHANTOM FOUNTAINS

While watching television one mild, dry October night in 1963, Francis Martin and his family noticed an expanding wet spot on the wall of their Methuen, Massachusetts, home. Then they heard a distinct popping sound, and watched a fountain of water spurt from the site. The water would flow for about twenty minutes, stop, and resume fifteen minutes later. During the succeeding days, the phenomenon spread to other sites around the house.

Soon the Martins' home was too waterlogged to inhabit and the family was forced to move in with Mrs. Martin's mother in nearby Lawrence. The phantom fountains, however, soon began occurring in the Lawrence house as well. The deputy fire chief, called in to thoroughly examine the pipes, was unable to find any leaks that might have caused the water flows, which he also witnessed.

Deciding to return to Methuen, Martin turned off the water main and drained all the pipes in their own house. Although the pipes were all in perfect repair, the flooding persisted. When the family relocated once more to Lawrence, the fountains followed too.

Eventually, the watery assaults ceased as mysteriously and suddenly as they had begun.

THE VISION OF CYRANO DE BERGERAC

Cyrano de Bergerac's legendary nose has been immortalized in many modern tales, but the French author's own tales deserve even greater attention. Few people are aware that the man may have been a prophet in his own right.

In his posthumously published tales of trips to the sun and moon, he described the orbits of the planets around the sun, which at that time was not a popularly accepted idea. He described a form of rocket propulsion. Cyrano also expressed the idea that traditional myths and religions were bequeathed to human beings by extraterrestrial visitors on earth.

The celestial travels of Cyrano's writings involved the use of an amazing array of apparatus unheard of in the seventeenth century. To his contemporaries, his ideas—which included movable dwellings, devices to record and replay speech, tubes that illuminate the dark—would certainly have seemed bizarre. Today, they seem remarkably similar to mobile homes, tape recorders, and light bulbs.

THE DOOM OF SEAFORTH

Bored with the tedious life at Brahan Castle, the earl of Seaforth packed his bags in 1660 and left for Paris where he would remain indefinitely. He didn't expect such an action to affect the entire Seaforth family line.

As each day passed and the earl had still not returned to Seaforth, his suspicious wife, Isabella, grew angrier. One evening, during a gathering of guests at the castle, she summoned Kenneth MacKenzie, a local seer known as the Warlock of the Glen whose abilities were known throughout the Scottish countryside. Gazing into the hole of a small white stone, he could foresee future events and had predicted, among other things, the bloody battle of Culloden Moor and other historic events.

Isabella, however, was not concerned about war and politics. She wanted to know what her husband was doing and where he was doing it. To answer her query, MacKenzie began to peer into his stone, only to soon begin laughing. With Isabella demanding to know what amused him, MacKenzie reluctantly replied that he had, indeed, perceived an image of the earl. Yes, he was still in Paris, he told her, and he was enjoying himself in the company of two beautiful young women, one sitting on his knee, the other stroking his hair. Humiliated in front of her guests, Isabella was furious and ordered the seer to be executed. But before he was put to death, MacKenzie placed a curse on Isabella and her family.

According to what became known as the Seaforth Doom, the Seaforth family line would eventually become extinct,

MacKenzie declared, detailing the fate that would befall the cursed descendants. The last living descendant would be deaf and mute, and he would outlive his four sons. Brahan Castle would end up in the hands of a woman, who would eventually be responsible for her sister's death. The Seaforth estate, moreover, would cease to exist.

In time, as the family continued to prosper, despite some minor setbacks during changing political climates, the curse was forgotten. Then in 1783, the only living Seaforth heir, Francis Humberston MacKenzie, inherited the castle and the estate. During childhood, the new master of Brahan Castle had contracted scarlet fever. As a result, he was deaf and mute, although he regained limited speech later in life, married, and fathered ten children, including four sons.

When Francis died in 1815, having outlived his four sons, there were no male heirs to the Seaforth title. The estate, then, went to the earl's daughter, Mary Elizabeth Frederica. Soon afterward, Mary took her younger sister Catherine out for a fateful carriage ride. During the excursion, one of the horses bolted and caused the entire team to run out of control, dragging the carriage along with them. The carriage hit a rock along the road, overturned, and rolled down a bank, killing Catherine almost instantly.

Eventually, devastated by financial mismanagement, extravagance, and government fines, Mary was forced to sell the Seaforth estate, piece by piece, until there was nothing left. With the land, the castle, and even the family name gone forever, the Seaforths were no more—just as the Warlock of the Glen had predicted.

REVENGE OF THE FISH

One of the favorite dishes among natives of Papua New Guinea, is needlefish, a thin, silvery, foot-long marine creature with a three-inch-long bony snout. But then the fish began attacking its potential captors—as many as twenty victims a month—in deadly fashion. And natives began calling on the spirit world for protection, chanting incantations as they sat in their boats waiting for a bite.

Physician Peter Barss first encountered the results of needlefish attacks a week after he began working at the Milne Bay Hospital. Villagers presented him with the body of a fisherman who had died when a sharp piece of bone pierced his chest. The source of the bone became evident a week later when the natives arrived with another dead fisherman. This time, the bone was still attached to its owner: a live needlefish imbedded in the man's stomach.

During the ensuing weeks, Barss saw numerous other cases of needlefish attacks, most of them occurring at night. Initially the doctor speculated that the fish were attracted by the light of the lanterns, somewhat like moths, and they had accidentally "stabbed" the unsuspecting fishermen. But there were other people who had been assaulted in broad daylight, including a three-year-old girl who was paralyzed as a result of a needlefish plunge. So Barss concluded that the fish were purposely hurling themselves at the occupants of fishing boats on a sort of kamikaze mission to exact revenge.

THE PHILADELPHIA
EXPERIMENT

In 1943 a top secret experiment at the U.S. Navy Yard in Philadelphia was designed to test the ultimate weapon: an invisible battleship. As a result, however, numerous people involved suffered bizarre aftereffects—most notably, spontaneous human combustion—and the government eventually canceled, and covered up, the project.

The Navy was using a powerful electromagnetic field (EMF) in its attempts to render the destroyer escort U.S.S. *Eldridge* invisible to radar and magnetic mines. During World War II, of course, scientists didn't understand the harmful effects EMFs could have on the central nervous system. Consequently, while working to make the ship invisible to detection, some crewmen may have inadvertently gotten too close to the source of the electromagnetic energy.

The Navy continues to deny there was ever such an experiment, claiming it was concocted by a 1955 book about UFOs. But the case files are still open and from time to time new evidence emerges.

BLIND VISION

People often recall previous lives in such detail that it's almost impossible to not accept reincarnation as fact. Science, however, demands evidence. If a person born blind had visual memories of a previous lifetime, philosophy professor James Parejko postulated, it would go a long way toward proof of reincarnation. To that end, he set up an experiment at Chicago State University to test his hypothesis.

Parejko began by hypnotizing three blind subjects and regressing them into past lives. Just as he had hoped, all three reported *seeing* things. They spoke, for example, of flickering candles, yellow teeth, and people with blotches on their faces. And their accounts indicated the reactions of a sighted person. In one case, a subject spoke about having to look away when the sun shone on the jewelry of another. Would a sightless person have any idea that such an action was necessary?

Parejko doesn't agree with skeptics who suggest that the three blind persons could easily have gotten their descriptions from books. He cites the case of a man who, once his sight was restored, was baffled by the difference between the way he had imagined things and what he actually saw. The blind, moreover, report that their past lives are much more vivid than their dreams.

THE QUEST FOR JASON

One of the greatest explorers in Greek mythology, Jason and his crew of Argonauts successfully battled such legendary foes as the Amazons and the half-bird, half-woman creatures known as Harpies in their quest for the Golden Fleece. Oxford University scholar Tim Severin believes Jason was much more than a fictional hero.

According to Severin, Jason lived during the Bronze Age, some three thousand years ago. Because the era lacks a written history, Severin decided to embark on an expedition to trace the Argonauts' ancient route and to gather archaeological evidence of Jason's existence.

Severin and a group of twenty colleagues set sail in March 1984 from Volos, Greece, in a ship the Oxford scholar christened *Argo* after Jason's famed vessel. Volos, of course, is said to be the site of Jason's home, the ancient city of Pegasae, and from there, Severin hoped to proceed through the Black Sea to find the kingdom of Colchis, the home of Jason's wife, the sorceress Medea, and believed to have been located somewhere near the modern Soviet republic of Georgia.

The evidence still hasn't been found, but Severin is confident that Soviet archaeologists will be able to provide concrete proof that Jason had, indeed, roamed the Georgian land in ancient times. After all, Severin points out, it's rare, if not unheard of, to have an epic that is entirely imaginary.

Tom Harper take note

GREAT BALLS OF FIRE

Except for thunderclouds some sixty miles away, the sky was clear as the Russian passenger plane departed the town of Sochi in 1984, and all signs pointed to a routine flight. Soon after they left the local airport, however, the pilots saw a glowing fireball, with a diameter of about four inches, outside the cockpit's window. With a deafening noise, the fireball suddenly shot through the metal wall of the fuselage and reappeared in the main section of the plane. The shocked passengers watched as it swooped over their heads and zipped toward the rear where it split into two crescent-shaped halves. In another moment, it had re-formed and exited through the rear, vanishing without a trace.

The pilots turned the plane around and headed directly back to Sochi, where investigators discovered that the plane's radar equipment had been severely damaged. There was a hole, moreover, in both the fuselage and the tail.

The fireball, Soviet scientists decided, was a rare and little understood phenomenon known as ball lightning, which years earlier was also experienced by a United States military plane. In a fashion similar to the Soviet experience, the fireball entered the cockpit, passed between the two astonished American pilots, drifted through the plane, and then shot out the back.

THE HUMAN LIGHTNING ROD

Most of us fear being struck by lightning during electrical storms, but the chances of that happening are, in fact, rather slim. Being struck more than once is even more improbable. For Betty Jo Hudson, however, the odds are much higher. The Winburn Chapel, Mississippi, woman has come to the conclusion that she's a human lightning rod.

Hudson first noticed her electrical affinity when she was a child and lightning struck her in the face. Not long afterward, her parents' home received a powerful electrical jolt and, in 1957, the house was completely destroyed by yet another lightning blast. When the woman married Ernest Hudson, however, the lightning seemed to change course. Her new home became the focus and was struck three times. Now, even the neighbors were being hit during electrical storms. And lightning has struck trees as well as a water pump in the yard. One bolt even killed the Hudson's dog.

One of the more recent episodes occurred when the Hudsons were shelling butter beans on their front porch one summer afternoon. A flash storm passed through, sending the couple scurrying inside. As they huddled together, they heard a horrifying crash: the lightning had devastated the bedroom.

Dying for Publicity

Some common motives for suicide are escape from sorrow or unbearable difficulties, protest, honor—fairly common in Japan and other parts of Asia—escape from incurable illness, and unrequited love, perhaps not now so common as it was in other, more romantic eras. But a recent offer by Portuguese poet Joaquim Castro Caldes to commit suicide for the sake of personal publicity is an interesting exception. He made the offer in good faith to the Gulbenkian Foundation, a world organization dedicated to the arts.

Castro offered to commit suicide for $7,000 (it sounds better in Portuguese currency—1,320,000 escudos). He even submitted a breakdown of how the money was to be spent on his commemorative funeral: 70,000 escudos for revolver and bullets; 500,000 for cremation and scattering of his ashes in the Tagus River flowing through Lisbon; 500,000 for a good orchestra to play Mahler's *Kindertotenlieder;* and 250,000 for an orchestrated performance by two hundred clowns.

Not surprisingly, the foundation refused the detailed and imaginative offer which nevertheless became known to the press, possibly through information furnished by the prospective "victim." In any case, the poet got the publicity he wanted, without having to kill himself for it.

CANINE HERO

When Christine Harrison visited her parents in Barnsley, England, she took along her Chihuahua, Percy. While there, Percy ran into the street and was hit by a car and, as far as anyone could tell, the dog was dead. The family wrapped the beloved pet in a heavy paper bag and buried it in a two-foot-deep grave in the backyard.

Christine's parents' dog, Mick, however, wouldn't leave the grave alone. The terrier frantically sniffed and scratched at the dirt, and began digging his way down. Finally unearthing the burial sack, Mick carried it into the house, where he began licking the Chihuahua. Percy, it seems, was unconscious but with a faint heartbeat.

The family rushed the Chihuahua to the veterinarian, who revived him and concluded that Percy had been in shock and survived under ground because of the air trapped in the paper bag. Mick's tongue massage, moreover, had stimulated the smaller dog's circulation.

Percy fully recovered, and the Royal Society for the Prevention of Cruelty to Animals awarded Mick an animal lifesaving award. What impressed Christine the most about the remarkable canine heroism, however, was the fact that the two dogs had always hated each other.

Storm Drain Crocodiles

Tales of alligators in New York City sewers have flourished for years, despite the lack of evidence. But in Cairns, Australia, three- to four-foot-long crocodiles often roam through sewers. Although the crocs rarely bother residents, at least one developed a taste for people.

One afternoon, twenty-one-year-old Leon Phillips was walking down the main street in Cairns, when a hefty crocodile stuck its head out of a sewer and grabbed the young man by the leg. Fortunately, Phillips was able to kick the crocodile away with his heavy cowboy boots and the help of a passing cab driver.

No one is quite sure how the crocodiles found their way into the sewer system, but some suggest that somebody may have had a small croc or two that grew too large and they released them into storm drains.

The Eye of the God

The medical symbol that looks like an R with a cross at the bottom that appears on doctors' prescriptions is not a letter at all. It is a shortened form of the hieroglyph for "eye"—specifically the eye of Horus, the

Egyptian god of medicine and cures. Adopted by doctors of ancient times as a symbol of their craft, its use has survived the civilization of pharaonic Egypt by thousands of years, and today, when doctors write prescriptions, they may not realize it, but they're paying homage to the god of medicine and cures.

THE ZOMBIE IN THE FIELDS

Zombies, legendary or not, are an accepted fact of life in Haiti. A possible explanation for so many cases of the seemingly dead and buried being brought back to life to do manual labor is that the so-called death is not really death but a deep coma deliberately induced by drugs. The designated victims, appearing to be dead, are buried, and then dug up, resuscitated by different drugs, and sold as field workers by the voodoo practitioners. A lady who lived on an estate in rural Haiti some years ago, Mrs. Gloria Andrulonis, had an unusual experience related to zombies when her cook's daughter died. The girl was duly buried but, a few days after the funeral, servants from the next estate told the cook that they had seen her daughter working in the fields of a neighboring plantation with a group of zombies.

When Mrs. Andrulonis asked her cook what she did about that fact, the woman replied, "Nothing. What can one do? She is dead. She has been buried and her soul has gone."

It is believed that zombies are supposed to be fed only unsweetened and unsalted food. A number of cases have been reported in Haiti about so-called zombies who ate sweets, remembered their death, and tried to go back to their graves.

THE MYSTERIOUS SOVIET MUMMIES

Soviet speleologists exploring caves in central Russia discovered a virtual city of the dead, composed of dozens of ancient, mummified men, horses, and wild animals. Soviet scientists speculate that the men had been fleeing the armies of Alexander the Great, who reached modern-day Afghanistan in the fourth century B.C. On the other hand, they could have been driven into the caves by a tribal feud and ended up meeting a mysterious collective death. Others, like Emory University anthropologist Brad Shore, believe that the men may have been the victims of a natural disaster: a mudslide or landslide could have trapped the victims, burying them alive and then preserving their bodies.

The mummies, however, also disclosed evidence of mite infestation that had left the men with painful body sores, which didn't surprise the mountain people who live in the area today. They have always believed that the black plague originated with mites from the nearby caves.

THE BEDSIDE BOMB

The Nazis were approaching the Soviet town of Berdyansk in 1941, heralding their arrival with gunfire and bombs. Zinaida Bragantsova sat by the window, sewing and trying to remain calm. Suddenly, a harsh blast of hot wind knocked the woman unconscious, and when she came to, she discovered a huge hole in the floor. Inside lay a German bomb. During the continued shelling, Bragantsova was unable to seek the help of authorities, so she simply patched up the floor and waited out the war.

For years afterward, Bragantsova pleaded with anyone who would listen, but no one would believe her story about a bomb under her bed. Her neighbors thought she was crazy. Soviet officials even accused the woman of fabricating the whole incident in order to get a new apartment.

In 1984, however, a telephone cable was being installed in Bragantsova's neighborhood and demolition experts were in Berdyansk to check for unexploded World War II bombs that might still be lying around. Bragantsova again pleaded for someone to remove her bomb. And this time an army lieutenant was sent to investigate. Sure enough, a five-hundred-pound German bomb was found in the hole now under the old woman's bed, which she had placed over the spot to hide the ugly patch work.

After the Berdyansk neighborhood was hastily evacuated, the bomb was detonated, destroying Bragantsova's home in the process. But the grandmother was finally rid of the bomb and would receive a new apartment.

*　　*　　*

The problem with a decades-old bomb is that, for no known reason, it can suddenly go off. Fortunately for Zinaida Bragantsova, the bomb under her bed waited forty-three years to be found before exploding.

THE PYRAMID AT THE
BOTTOM OF THE SEA

East of the Florida Keys, about twenty-seven miles north of Cuba at a depth of one thousand feet, a pyramidal formation rises from the sea bottom. It is so regularly shaped that it appears to be a man-made construction. Its height, as indicated on the radar screen, appears to be about four hundred feet, making it comparable to the pyramids of Egypt. If this is in fact a pyramid it would be one more proof of the existence of a now submerged ancient culture whose ruined buildings, roads, stone walls, stairways, and shaped monoliths are scattered along the seafloors of the Caribbean and the western Atlantic. These would be the remnants of settlements covered by the ocean when the ocean rose and the land sank during the earth and sea changes that occurred at the end of the Third Glaciation more than ten thousand years ago.

The huge stone formation or man-made pyramid was outlined in the 1970s by a fishing captain, John Henry, using sonar to track schools of fish. It is located not on the Bahama Banks but on the ocean floor, after dropping off in the vicinity of Cay Sal.

According to the sonar image, its top is several hundred feet below the surface, making it impossible for scuba divers to examine it in sufficient detail.

Its profile, although regular, does not resemble an Egyptian pyramid but rather an Aztec or Mayan one with a small construction at its flattened summit. It has been researched and photographed by several expeditions. Photographs and films from lowered cameras have been taken by researchers Jacques Mayol and Ari Marshall. These photographs indicate the curious presence of flashing globules of light at the lower section of the pyramidal mass.

About ten years ago, according to the account of several crew members, the U.S. atomic submarine they were on was cruising near the bottom of what they referred to as the "Bermuda Triangle," when it struck something solid. The submarine personnel were not hurt and the submarine, which had ice-breaking equipment, was not damaged. Depth maps showed no underwater cliffs or mountains in the area but sonar mapping might easily miss a pyramidal formation even if crossing it at a lower level.

Since no further information was released by official sources we are left with only an intriguing concept. Perhaps man's most modern and perfected underwater combat vehicle collided with a pyramid so old that the land it was built on has since sunk beneath the sea.

NEAR-DEATH EXPERIENCES OF HELL

Near-death experiences, in which individuals report leaving their bodies and heading toward a bright light, are an increasingly recognized phenomenon. But according to Maurice Rawlings, clinical professor of medicine at the

University of Tennessee College of Medicine in Chatta-
nooga, some of the trips to the outskirts of heaven may
possibly be glimpses into hell.

Rawlings interviewed nearly three hundred patients immediately after their resuscitations. And the stories he heard
from at least half of them convinced him that they'd seen
lakes of fire and demonic figures, not the benevolent images
reported in better known near-death stories. Rawlings believes that many people substantially alter their accounts
simply because they're ashamed to admit they might not be
going to heaven.

ALIEN JUMP START

On a Sunday night in November 1976, Joyce
Bowles and her neighbor Ted Pratt were driving to the
British village of Chilcomb to pick up Bowles's son. On the
way, the car began to shake violently and careened on to the
grassy shoulder alongside the road. The engine inexplicably
stopped running and the headlights blacked out.

Then Bowles and Pratt saw the glowing, orange cigar-
shaped craft hovering over the road near them. Through a
window in the side of the vehicle, Bowles and Pratt saw
three heads lined up as if they were passengers on a bus.

One of the mysterious ship's occupants emerged and approached the humans. The creature was wearing a silver
jumpsuit and had intense pink eyes without pupils or irises,
Bowles later reported. "He peered through the window at
the dashboard controls," Bowles recalled. When he did so,
the engine fired and the headlights flashed back on. "Then,
he and the cigar simply vanished."

Some experts believe that the point of encounter was especially attractive to extraterrestrials. It lies at an intersection of a grid of lines drawn between local ancient burial grounds.

THE RESILIENT BRAIN

While the brain is considered our most delicate organ, there have been numerous recorded cases of injury to the brain that mysteriously had no adverse effects on the patient. One such incident involved a young mill worker who, in 1879, was struck above her right eye by a machine bolt. The impact of the bolt drove bone fragments four inches into the woman's brain, destroying bits of it in the process. Subsequent surgery, moreover, resulted in even more physical damage to the organ. Yet the woman recovered fully, not even suffering a headache during the next forty-two years of her life.

The brain of Phineas Gage, however, was perhaps one of the most remarkably resilient of all time. A twenty-five-year-old railroad foreman, Gage was ramming explosive material into a hole on September 13, 1847, using a long metal rod with a sharp point at one end. When the bar struck a rock, it created a spark and during the subsequent explosion, the rod shot through Gage's cheekbone with bulletlike speed. Nearly forcing his eye out of its socket, the rod went straight through the man's skull, with about eighteen inches protruding from the top of his head.

Amazingly, Gage did not lose consciousness as he was rushed to a hotel where they could summon a doctor. On his arrival, Gage got up and walked into the building. The doctor called in a surgeon who removed the bar, extracting bits of bone and brain with it. Although neither physician expected Gage to live, he astounded all the medical authorities who examined him. He miraculously recovered suffering only the loss of vision in his left eye.

DREAMS THAT COME TRUE

While there are those who doubt the veracity of prophetic dreams, many people have foreseen the future during their sleep. Author Rudyard Kipling, for example, reported a dream in which he was at a formal event. His view of an unidentifiable ceremony was obstructed by the belly of a fat man in front of him. And at the end of the dream, a stranger approached and asked to have a word with Kipling. Six weeks later, Kipling was at an affair that he soon recognized as the one he'd attended in his dream. The entire event, in fact, was exactly the same as he had seen it, including the details of the fat man and the stranger.

There have been countless ordinary people who have also shared a vision of the future in their dreams. Four-year-old Robert Beresford of Buckinghamshire, England, wasn't exactly concerned about World War I in October 1918. But on the eighteenth of the month, while taking his afternoon nap, he began muttering in his sleep. "Poor Mrs. Timms," Robert's parents heard him saying. "Won't someone please tell her?" While the boy still lay sleeping, they asked him what they should tell Mrs. Timms. "It's about Edwin," he replied after several minutes. He's dead, dead in the mud." The parents were baffled. They knew no one named Timms or Edwin. When he awoke, Robert remembered nothing about the dream.

Having mentioned the episode to the family doctor, he recalled a woman named Mrs. Timms who lived about twenty miles away. When he inquired, he learned that she, in fact, had a son named Edwin stationed in France. On the day of the dream, Edwin had been killed in battle. Robert Beresford had obviously reported Edwin's death even before his mother had received official notification.

Helen Watson of Ellerbuck, England, also experienced a prophetic wartime dream, involving her son, Teddy, who had been among the missing since the 1940 battle at Dunkirk. Many vital records had been destroyed during the evacuation of Dunkirk and there had never been official documentation of where Teddy had been buried. One night in 1956, however, Helen dreamed she was in a military cemetery at Dunkirk amid rows and rows of unmarked white crosses. As she approached one particular gravesite, her son appeared, smiled at her, and then disappeared.

Afterward, when she traveled to the Dunkirk cemetery, Helen Watson found the gravesite her son had indicated in the dream. She contacted officials who agreed to exhume the coffin. Inside, they found the rosary, locket, and monogrammed cigarette holder belonging to Corporal Teddy Watson.

OPTICAL ANOMALIES

A legendary one-eyed giant, the figure of the Cyclops appears in myths throughout the world. But a man living in a Mississippi backwoods community may have been the first truly one-eyed human being. His single orb, completely normal in every regard, was located in the center of his forehead, according to the *Boston Medical Journal*. And for years, sideshow and circus promoters pursued the man, but he adamantly refused to become a public spectacle.

The Mississippi man, of course, isn't the only person in the world to have ever endured an anomalous collection of eyes. There was an English four-eyed man, for example, who could open and close each eye independently and look in four different directions at once.

THE RETIREMENT OF A MONSTER LOBSTER

When physician George Macris of Palmer, Alaska, was out shopping for lobster, a favorite local dish, to serve at an upcoming dinner party, he came upon a monstrous beauty in his grocery store's tank. Macris, a long-time lobster diver, had never seen one like it before: it was more than three feet long and had claws "the size of catchers' mitts." And Macris, a marine biology hobbyist, knew it was a perfect genetic specimen of a nearly ninety-year-old arthropod. He knew the fate of a lobster that size would have to change. So he bought the old lobster to save it from being boiled to death.

Macris subsequently purchased a one-way plane ticket to Maine, where state law prohibits the capture of lobsters that are larger than those usually found. He then packed his enormous charge, dubbed Monster Mike, in ice and saline-soaked rags, and drove through freezing rain to the airport. Although Monster Mike later missed the connecting flight in Chicago, it arrived in Portland, Maine, twenty-four hours after departing Alaska and was met by marine patrol lieutenant Joseph Fessenden. The following day, Fessenden dropped the lobster off at the mouth of Portland harbor, where it has been ever since, enjoying a protected old age.

THE SHIPWRECKED WOMAN AND THE GIANT TURTLE

Candlearia Villanueva was traveling on the *Aloha* when it caught fire and sank six hundred miles south of Manila. A life jacket strapped around her body, the woman floated in the sea for more than twelve hours before a giant sea turtle appeared beneath her. Some thirty-six hours later, the crew of a Philippine navy vessel rescued her, thinking the woman was clinging to an oil drum. They didn't realize that the turtle was holding her afloat until after they pulled the woman on board. Villanueva later reported that there was also another, smaller turtle that had crawled up on her back and seemed to bite her every time she was about to fall asleep. She thought that, perhaps, it wanted to prevent her from submerging her head in the water and drowning.

THE CEMENT PILLARS OF NEW CALEDONIA

As far as anyone knows, the first human visitors to New Caledonia, about 750 miles east of Australia, arrived from Indonesia around 2000 B.C., which is why archaeologists have a hard time explaining the odd presence of cement pillars. Perhaps tens of thousands of years old, the pillars lie on the New Caledonian Isle of Pines, some forty miles off the southern coast.

Scientists had known about the Isle of Pines' some four hundred tumuli, the anthill-shaped land formations, eight to nine feet high, three hundred feet in diameter, and virtually bare of vegetation. It was during eventual excavation of the geological curiosities during the sixties by L. Chevalier of the Museum of New Caledonia at Nouméa, the island's capital, that one cement pillar was unexpectedly found in each of three tumuli, and two lying side by side in a fourth. Their heights ranged from forty to one hundred inches, and their diameters from forty to seventy-five inches. They were made, strangely enough, with a lime and mortar mixture, a procedure unheard of before a few hundred years B.C. Even so, based on radiocarbon dating, the pillars were created between 5120 and 10,950 B.C.

What Chevalier found most baffling about the find, however, was that there were no human remains found anywhere around the site. Given the apparent age of the cylinders, the absence of nearby human or other life, and the sophistication of their construction, the origins of the pillars remains a complete mystery.

THE HOUSE ON HAUNTED HILL

During the excavation of their backyard for a swimming pool, Sam and Judy Haney unearthed two dead bodies. But that was only the beginning of their problems. It wasn't long before the television was glowing even when it was turned off; sparks flew from unplugged clocks; and shoes disappeared, being found later on top of one of the graves in the backyard.

The Haneys' home and others like it in the suburban development, it turned out, were built over a nineteenth-century cemetery. And disturbances have also affected some of the other homeowners: cups have broken while sitting on shelves, appliances stop working with no apparent cause, and lights and water faucets have mysteriously turned on. An apparition, known as Betty, has appeared and frightened some residents away.

Claiming mental anguish and stress-induced diabetes, the Haneys sued the developer for $2 million. The jury recommended a settlement of $142,000, but the judge overturned the jury's decision and awarded the Haneys nothing. The developer had not been negligent, the judge decreed, and had not intentionally misled them about the presence of the graves.

The Haneys subsequently moved and there's been no mention of an appeal.

SPONTANEOUS HUMAN COMBUSTION INSIDE PARKED CARS

Two of the most unusual cases of spontaneous human combustion occurred while the victims sat inside their automobiles. The first occurred in December 1959 and was initially dismissed as a suicide. A despondent autoworker in Pontiac, Michigan, Billy Peterson had indeed bent his car's exhaust pipe to lead into the front seat, and the official cause of death was listed as carbon monoxide poisoning. But doctors were unable to explain the third-degree burns on the body's back, legs, and arms, especially since his clothing— even his underwear—had not been burned. They were even more baffled by the fact that hairs on the charred parts of the body were not even singed.

In October 1964, seventy-five-year-old Olga Worth Stephens of Dallas, Texas, was sitting in her parked car when, according to eyewitnesses, she suddenly burst into flames. By the time rescuers arrived on the scene, Stephens had been burned beyond recognition, yet nothing else in the car had been affected. The subsequent investigators were unable to explain the fatal fire.

DWELLERS ON THE MOON

In 1835, the *New York Sun* published a purely imaginative series of articles that gave readers their first glimpse of life on the moon. Entitled "Great Astronomical Discoveries Largely Made by Sir John Herschel at the Cape of Good Hope," the articles were based on statements attributed to the world-famous astronomer, which gave credence to the speculations.

Herschel, the reporter Richard Locke claimed, had used a new seven-ton telescope located at the Cape of Good Hope in South Africa to view the surface of the moon in greater detail than had ever been possible. Magnifying the moon by forty-two thousand times, and bringing it into sight within the equivalent of 5 miles, Herschel was able to clearly see mountains of amethyst and beaches along great lakes, the largest being 266 miles long. By adjusting the telescope's lens, Herschel could focus on the surface within eighty yards and observe an array of creatures, including blue, single-horned goats, huge cranes and other birds, as well as beasts that resembled American buffalo and bears. He could even identify species of trees. Most surprising of all, he had witnessed four-foot-tall humanoid creatures with wings and monkeylike faces roaming the lunar surface.

The New York Times editorialized that the Great Astronomical Discoveries series displayed "the most extensive and accurate knowledge of astronomy." And the reports, later compiled and published in a separate pamphlet and sold on newsstands, resulted in the newspaper's circulation increasing by 650 percent.

The truth wasn't revealed until Locke admitted to another

newspaperman that he had, in fact, fabricated the entire series. When the news appeared in the *Journal of Commerce*, thousands of credulous people were disappointed. Herschel, however, thought it was a great joke.

THE WINNING ENTRY

When the German magazine *Das Beste* ran a reader competition in 1979, the editors had no idea that the winning entry would reveal a bizarre coincidence. Responding to the contest for the most interesting personal experience, a pilot named Walter Kellner of Munich, West Germany, submitted his story of survival. He had been flying a Cessna 421 over the Tyrrhenian Sea between Sardinia and Sicily, he wrote, when the plane experienced engine trouble. Plunging into the sea, he survived by floating in a rubber dinghy until he was rescued.

Impressed by the tale, the *Das Beste* editors placed Kellner's account among the competition's finalists. They then set out to confirm the incident with German and Italian officials. Kellner's personal story was true in every detail and was named the winner in the magazine's contest.

The competition results were announced and Kellner was to be awarded his prize on December 6. That day, however, *Das Beste* editor-in-chief Wulf Schwarzwaller received a strange letter from a Walter Kellner of Kritzendorf, Austria, who claimed the German Kellner's story as his own, although it had a different ending. According to the Austrian Kellner, he had been flying his Cessna 421 over the Tyrrhenian Sea when engine trouble forced him to land at Cagliari airstrip in Sardinia. The second Kellner accused the first pilot of being an impostor and said that his personal story was a hoax.

The first Walter Kellner admitted that he was aware, from the plane's records, that another pilot named Kellner had flown the same Cessna but, he said, he hadn't known they shared the same first name and had experienced similar mechanical failures while flying over the same location.

With further checking, the editors learned that *both* stories were indeed true.

THE GHOSTS OF LONDON TOWER

In 1605, Henry Percy, ninth earl of Cumberland, was sentenced to London's Martin Tower for his involvement in the Gunpowder Plot to blow up Parliament and with it King James I. The earl remained there for sixteen years before buying his freedom for thirty thousand pounds. Even though he was released and never executed, his ghost has haunted the Tower ever since his death and has been seen walking the battlements where Percy often took the air during his imprisonment.

Lady Jane Grey, of course, was an even more illustrious resident of the Tower, sentenced for her roll in an abortive attempt to become queen of England. On February 12, 1554, she was beheaded on the grounds outside the Tower and her ghost has haunted the edifice ever since. As recently as 1957, on the anniversary of her death, a Tower guard saw a white mass form into the image of Lady Jane. He immediately called another guard, who also saw the apparition.

While Martin Tower is rich in spectral lore, not all of it involves the ghosts of former prisoners, one of the strangest apparently appearing only once and defying all efforts to explain it. In October 1817, Edmund Lenthal Swifte, keeper of the crown jewels, was dining with his family in Martin Tower, where the jewels were then stored. When they suddenly looked up from their meal, they saw a glass cylinder filled with a swirling blue and white liquid hovering just above the table. It slowly moved behind Swifte's wife who began screaming. When Swifte threw a chair at the spectral container it disappeared and was never seen again.

Beginning with the reign of Henry I, moreover, the Tower was often used to house a collection of animals ranging from lions, tigers, and bears to monkeys, zebras, hyenas, and even elephants, collected for royal entertainment. The practice ceased in 1835 when a Tower guard was mauled by a lion. Before that, however, a Tower sentry was patrolling the entrance in 1815 when, on the stroke of midnight, he saw a huge bear rising on its hind legs in front of him. Terrified, the guard lunged with his bayonet, only to watch in amazement as it passed through nothingness and lodged in the oak door where the bear had been. The sentry reported the incident the following morning, but died the day after that, some say from shock.

ACCIDENTAL COINCIDENCE

On a June night in the thirties, El Paso, Texas, highway patrolman Allan Falby was pursuing a speeding truck. When the vehicle slowed down as it went around a corner, Falby's car plowed into it at full speed. His leg spurting blood from a ruptured artery, Falby would surely have died had it not been for Alfred Smith, a passerby who stopped to assist him. Smith applied a tourniquet to the patrolman's leg to curb the flow of blood until the ambulance arrived.

Five years after his near-fatal accident, Falby responded to a radio call for assistance at the scene of a one-car collision. The car had crashed head-on into a tree and the unconscious driver had severed an artery in his leg. Recalling his first aid training, Falby quickly applied a tourniquet, thus saving the man's life. Then on closer inspection, he realized that the injured driver was none other than Alfred Smith, the same man who had saved his life five years before.

REVITALIZING DECAPITATED HEADS

The guillotine was the preferred instrument of execution in nineteenth-century France. And the decapitations provided a bounty of severed heads in 1887 for one enterprising scientist to attempt attaching the heads to the bodies of dogs. Although the gruesome series of experiments failed, modern researchers believe it may soon be possible to revive a detached head and perhaps someday even organically grow an entirely new body for it.

In his book entitled *If We Can Keep a Severed Head Alive . . .* , attorney and engineer Chet Fleming cites one Cleveland experiment in 1971 in which severed monkey heads regained consciousness for thirty-six hours. Fleming has even patented a blood-processing system used for perfusing animal heads to keep them alive. He is quick to point out that no one can use his procedure without his permission. He wants to make sure that scientists work on live, severed heads with full regard for the ethical, legal, and social issues involved.

Some scientists are actually looking at the possibility of preserving heads for future use. Since cloning technology may be possible around the same time as viable cryonics (the freezing and later restoration to life of animals as well as human beings), they'll be able to clone a new body for the frozen head.

ANCIENT AND MODERN CANNIBALS

Modern anthropologists hold that tales of cannibalism among primitive tribes is largely myth. But evidence unearthed by archaeologist Jean Courtin indicates that as far back as the Stone Age at least one group of Stone Age dwellers did, in fact, eat human flesh.

Investigating a cave near Fontgregoua in southeastern France, Courtin and his colleagues found the remains of six humans who had been dead for some six thousand years. When closely examined, the bones revealed tiny cuts and chop marks. The flesh of the deceased had apparently been systematically stripped from their bones.

While it doesn't prove that whoever removed the flesh actually ate it, Courtin's find at least indicates that same-species butchering with some sort of tool had taken place.

Anthropologist Paola Villa, who examined the bones, believes that the six skeletons may have been prisoners of war killed and eaten by their captors.

The word "cannibal" comes from *caribal* which refers to the eating habits of certain of the Caribbean Indians as observed by Columbus when he first arrived there.

There have been many reasons for cannibalism. One group in the islands of the South Pacific used to eat the heart and other body parts of their enemies, to absorb their bravery and force. In other areas as far apart as Ireland and China, cannibalism has occurred sporadically during the great famines of the 1840s (Ireland) and the 1930s (China). A number of incidents of cannibalism have taken place at sea among survivors of shipwrecks and other disasters who were stranded without food.

The Aztecs, as noted by the Spanish conquistadores when they first arrived in Mexico, limited their cannibalism to eating the arms and legs (often cooked in *mole*, a spicy chocolate sauce) of the captives sacrificed to the gods on the altars at the top of their lofty pyramidal temples. They gave the torso of the victim to the animals in the imperial zoo but kept the heads for decorating a special building in front of the main temple in what is now Mexico City.

Cannibalism continued to be practiced in the deep jungles of South America, New Guinea, and parts of central Africa until well into the twentieth century. An American author and explorer, William Seabrook, in describing an encounter with ritual cannibalism in Africa, wrote that he was offered some of the meat by a tribal chief. He deemed it was politic to accept, and like a true researcher, tried portions of it fried, stewed, and roasted. He found the roasted samples to be the best, and wrote that it tasted like pork. In this he agreed with the former cannibals of the South Seas, who referred to human meat as "long pig."

REINCARNATED PRODIGIES

There has been intense debate over the years about the source of child prodigies' incredible talents. Most psychologists contend that children like Wolfgang Amadeus Mozart, who was composing complex music at the age of five, are simply born with extraordinary memory and organizational skills. Others, however, believe that because their apparently learned abilities appear so early in their young lives, these amazing children are the product of reincarnation.

As evidence that the abilities are talents displayed in previous existences, proponents point to the cases of an eighteenth-century French boy, Jean Cardiac—who could recite the alphabet at the age of three months and spoke half a dozen languages by the time he was six years old—and a nineteenth-century blind four-year-old slave in Georgia called Blind Tom. According to one teacher, Tom could expertly play the piano the first time he tinkered the keys and "knew more of music than we know or can learn."

THE DREAM STORIES OF
ROBERT LOUIS STEVENSON

Robert Louis Stevenson always admitted that the plots of his popular stories were derived from dreams. He even claimed to dream plots at will. Early in his career, he wrote a story about dual personality—one good, one evil—entitled "The Traveling Companion." The story was summarily rejected by an editor who said that the idea was ingenious, but the plot was weak. Frustrated by his inability to improve the story, Stevenson decided to try dreaming up a solution. Blessed with extraordinary recall, he was able to remember every detail of his newly dreamed plot. And as he wrote what he had dreamed, "The Traveling Companion" was transformed into the classic *Dr. Jekyll and Mr. Hyde*.

THE GRIM PUN OF QIN
SHI-HUANG-DI

The Great Wall of China, built two thousand years ago, is the largest single artifact on earth and is also the only man-made construction visible from space, as noted by the first astronauts.

The more than twenty-five-hundred-mile length of wall represented an enormous cost in human life. But spending lives did not greatly concern the emperor, Qin Shi-Huang-di, whose purpose was to strengthen the northern borders of China. On the emperor's orders, slaves, prisoners, farmers, soldiers and, as a gesture of the emperor's contempt for any learning that predated *him,* a number of scholars and historians toiled and died building the wall. As the death toll mounted, a frightening prophecy was passed along the wall—ten thousand people would be buried in the wall before it was finished.

When the emperor learned of the prophecy, he said, "We will fulfill the prophecy," adding that everyone would then cease to worry and be able to work even harder. For he found a man named Wan whose name meant "ten thousand" and had him buried within the "Ten Thousand Mile Wall," or as it is called in Chinese, *Wan-li Chang-Ching.* Thus the name of the wall still contains the name of Wan, as well as Wan's skeleton along with an estimated ten times ten thousand other skeletons.

CHESAPEAKE UFO

Captain William Nash and his copilot William Fortenberry were making a routine New York to Miami run in a Pan American DC-4 around 8:00 P.M. on July 14, 1952. The sky was clear and visibility was unlimited, a perfect night for flying at an altitude of eight thousand feet.

Then, near Norfolk, Virginia, Nash and Fortenberry noticed an eerie glow not far off. It became apparent that the light was emanating from six fiery red objects, each about a hundred feet in diameter, and flying in formation. "Their shape was clearly outlined and evidently circular," Nash reported. "The edges were well defined, not phosphorescent or fuzzy in the least."

Flying about two thousand feet above Chesapeake Bay, the six discs were then joined by two others. And when they were nearly aligned below the DC-4, the lights dimmed slightly and the craft flipped on their sides.

The DC-4 flight team radioed a report to be forwarded to the U.S. Air Force, and the next morning were told that at least seven other groups in the area had reported the same glowing discs. But after checking the positions of all known military and civilian craft in the vicinity at that time, the Air Force was unable to account for what the UFOs might have been. The case remains in the Air Force files, classified as officially "unexplained."

1961 "Day the Earth Stood Still"

HEAVENLY MUSIC

The spirit of Franz Liszt is said to have appeared to Rosemary Brown in 1964, keeping a promise he had made to her many years before when she was only seven years old. He returned to give her his music. But he also brought the spirits of Chopin, Schubert, Schumann, Beethoven, Bach, Mozart, Brahms, and many others. Each of them asked her to transcribe their music composed after death. Her cupboards and drawers were soon overflowing with more than five hundred pieces of music.

"The music is absolutely in the style of these composers," insisted concert pianist Hephzibah Menuhin, Yehudi's sister, who agreed with many critics. And according to composer Richard Rodney Bennett, "A lot of people can improvise, but you couldn't fake music like this without years of training," which Brown had had extremely little of. (In fact, she attended the opera as a child against her will.)

Brown, however, does profess a strong background in psychic phenomena. Both her parents and her grandparents were psychic, and Brown became aware of her own ability when she was very young. In fact, by the time she was seven and Liszt first appeared to her, she was already accustomed to being visited by spirits.

As for her channeling the music of many of the world's greatest composers, musicians and psychologists have investigated Brown and they all have agreed there was no way that she could be cheating.

CRIMES OF PSYCHIC VISION

When Lockheed shipping clerk Etta Louise Smith heard a radio broadcast about a house-to-house search for a missing nurse, she immediately thought, *She's not in the house*. Then she received a visual picture, as if there were a photograph in front of her, and Smith knew the nurse was dead.

Then the thirty-nine-year-old mother of three went to the police station to speak with the investigators. From there she went out to a remote canyon site she'd also visualized. There she found the body of thirty-one-year-old Melanie Uribe.

But twelve hours later, Smith was arrested on suspicion of murder. During her four-hour stint in jail, however, one of the killers was arrested. He confessed and implicated two accomplices, who were also arrested and later convicted. And Smith went on to sue the city of Los Angeles for false arrest.

The judge ruled that the police had not lacked probable cause as well as sufficient evidence to implicate Smith in the murder. And the jury awarded her more than twenty-six thousand dollars. Still the police as well as the attorney representing the city continue to doubt that Smith had had a psychic experience and insist that somehow she had heard about it, perhaps through talk in the neighborhood.

THE REINCARNATION OF A MINISTER'S WIFE

Married to a minister and the mother of four children, Dolores Jay doesn't believe in reincarnation, neither speaks nor understands German, and has never even been to Germany. But when the American housewife is hypnotized she regresses in time, past her childhood and her infancy, until she suddenly becomes an adolescent girl in nineteenth-century Germany who remembers her dolls, her home, and her own death.

As sixteen-year-old Gretchen Gottlieb, she is terrified, hiding from anti-Catholics who have already killed her mother. Her head aches. She mumbles in German, mentions a gleaming knife, but desperately evades questions. She finally wails. And there it ends. Jay doesn't recall anything else until her own birth in 1923.

The Gretchen Gottlieb home was in Eberswalde, a small

town in what is now East Germany, close to the Polish border. During World War II, it was the site of the Germans' last stand against the Russians who almost completely razed it. Any records that may have proven the existence of Gretchen have been destroyed.

MUTILATED FARM ANIMALS

Throughout 1988, something vicious and deadly was mutilating farm animals in the southwest Alabama town of Geneva. Despite the fact that more than forty animals have been killed—including a horse whose genitals were ripped off and pigs whose entrails were torn out of their bodies—no one has been able to spot the creature responsible.

Among the casualties were several 60-pound pigs and a 250-pound boar owned by the Stinson family. "Whatever it is, it seems more interested in tearing its prey apart than in eating it," says Lance Stinson, whose parents and sister think they may have heard the killer one night. "They heard a high-pitched scream—it seemed to come from different directions at the same time."

According to Dot Kirkland, spokeswoman for the Geneva County Sheriff's Department, an official investigation of the mysterious animal deaths was hampered by droves of sightseers bent on catching a glimpse of the unknown killer. "We couldn't tell if there were any tracks because so many people were walking around out there," she says. "No new evidence has turned up and the killings seem to have stopped. We now think the animals were probably attacked by wild dogs."

Lance Stinson isn't so sure. "Some old-timers think it could be an injured, crazed bear. Others think it's a panther or even wolves," he says. "One thing is apparent, though. By the marks on our dead animals, whatever killed them had four claws on one foot and only three on the other. The Sheriff's department may believe dogs did this. But a lot of other people aren't convinced."

INTRADIMENSIONAL
TRAVELING MAYA

Mayan culture has always been an enigma for researchers who can't understand why a Stone Age society would have such an astute knowledge and understanding of mathematics, astronomy, and recorded time.

One theory, explains Colorado art historian José Argüelles, is that the Maya were intradimensional travelers who settled in Mexico around 600 B.C. Their mission: to place earth and its solar system in alignment with the universe.

Argüelles was first confronted with the idea of the Mayan travelers when he met a Mayan holy man who told him our solar system is the seventh one the Maya navigated. The leaders departed in the ninth century A.D., leaving behind their sacred calendar as a system of prophecy. And when the Mayan calendar ends in 2012, moreover, mankind will shift to a decentralized, nonindustrial culture in which contact with alien beings is commonplace.

THE MOTHER OF US ALL

According to the Bible, the first woman was Eve, Adam's mate and the mother of Cain and Abel, the matriarch of mankind. Some scholars, however, have considered Eve, as well as Adam, of course, to be merely representational of the beginnings of the human race. But a recent study at the University of California, Berkeley, actually traces modern humans to a single ancestor, a woman who lived in Africa some 200,000 years ago.

The single-ancestor theory is based on the study of DNA from the mitochrondrion—the part of the cell that converts food into energy—in 147 people. Biochemist Mark Stoneking at the University of California at Berkeley mapped the DNA, which is passed on only by the female of a species, and traced it backward in time. Estimating the mutation rate, he then determined that not only would the common ancestor be a female, but that she would have lived between 140,000 and 280,000 years ago.

CHRISTMAS COMBUSTION

In 1885, Patrick Rooney and his wife invited their son John and their hired hand, John Larson, to join them for a Christmas Eve drink. The four sat around the kitchen table, enjoying the whiskey Patrick had bought in town.

After a few shots of the liquor, young Rooney headed back to his own farm a mile away, and Larson retired to his room, leaving the hosts to finish off the bottle.

Larson rose before dawn, even though it was Christmas morning, to perform his routine chores. But when he walked into the kitchen, he found Patrick Rooney slumped in the chair where he'd been sitting the night before. He was dead. And Mrs. Rooney was nowhere to be found. In a daze, Larson raced to John's farm. When the two men returned to the death scene, they discovered a three- by four-foot hole in the floor. At the bottom lay the remains of the two-hundred-pound Mrs. Rooney: a burned piece of skull, two charred vertebrae, and a foot in a pile of ashes. She had evidently burned to death, the two men concluded. But why had nothing else in the kitchen been burned? And what had killed Patrick Rooney?

When the police and the coroner arrived, suspicion quickly fell on Larson, but no case could be made against him. The rising soot, they found, had left an outline of Larson's head on the pillow while he obviously slept through the ordeal. The coroner concluded that Mrs. Rooney had been the victim of spontaneous human combustion. Her husband, he suspected (and the jury agreed), had been asphyxiated by the fumes rising from his wife's burning body.

THE WOMAN WHO WAS
RESURRECTED BY THE MAN
SHE LOVED

Young, beautiful, and born into French nobility, Victorine Lefourcade was in love with a poor journalist named Julius Bossuet whom her parents refused to allow her to marry. Instead, they forced her to wed a man of their choosing, someone of appropriate class and status. It was a loveless marriage in which Victorine seemed to be a grieving widow and in 1810, after several years of misery, she became ill and died.

When Bossuet heard about her death, he traveled to the village graveyard where his beloved was buried. Desperately wanting a remembrance, some token that he could hold dear to him for the rest of his life, he began digging out the woman's coffin to snip a lock of her hair. As he began to cut the hair, however, Victorine opened her eyes.

As far as everyone else was concerned, Victorine was dead. So the two lovers remained hidden until Victorine regained her health, and they then sailed for the United States. Some twenty years later, confident no one would recognize the woman, the couple returned to France.

Someone did recognize her, however, and word soon got to her husband in her former life. Although he had Victorine arrested, the court refused to honor his claim against her and Victorine and Julius Bossuet were free to remain together and live in France.

STOCK MARKET PSYCHICS

Organized by clinical psychologist Judith Kuriansky and the editor of *Forbes* magazine, William Flanagan, the three-hour cruise uniting 120 stock market experts with 5 professional psychics was intended initially as a lark. According to Flanagan, he thought it might be an amusing way to "pick up on the vibrations and energy levels coming from Wall Street." But the East River cruise turned spooky when every one of the psychics reported negative energies pouring from downtown New York City. One psychic, a woman named Wendy, was convinced that at least two years of economic turmoil were forthcoming, with the Dow Jones average dropping as low as 1100 by the end of 1989. Her prediction, however, was in direct contrast to the current market analysis, which was overwhelmingly bullish. Even so, a week after the cruise, in October 1987, the financial world was devastated by Black Monday, when the market plummeted over 500 points.

AMELIA EARHART: LOST AMERICAN HEROINE

One of the most celebrated disappearances in recent history involved pilot and American heroine Amelia Earhart. Earhart and her copilot, Fred Noonan, took off from California on May 20, 1937, commencing what was to be an eastward circumnavigation of the globe. The flight was carefully tracked as the flight team passed over Florida, Brazil, Africa, India, and Australia in the specially equipped twin-engine plane.

On July 2, Earhart and Noonan refueled in Lae, New Guinea, and resumed their flight, intending a rendezvous with the Coast Guard ship *Itasca* in the central Pacific. The last transmission received from the pair, however, was confusing and fragmentary. No further messages went out over the radio, and the plane was never seen again.

Frantic searches were conducted, even employing George Putnam, a friend of Earhart and her husband. According to psychic Jacqueline Cochran, soon after losing contact Earhart was alive on an unidentified Pacific island. There was some speculation that the plane had gone down on a volcanic island that was subsequently submerged (or sank). Other possibilities included their capture by the Japanese who summarily executed her as a spy. In any case, no trace of the pilots or the aircraft has ever been found.

BRAINS THAT BAFFLED MEDICINE

   The brain is so complicated that scientists are constantly working to discover just how it works. It is well known, however, that even seemingly minor injuries and shocks can sometimes cause damage to the brain—and result in everything from a loss of sensation to seizures. On the other hand, medical literature cites cases of severe brain damage that didn't seem to faze patients at all.

   In 1879, for instance, a woman working in a mill suffered a ghastly on-the-job accident. A machine threw a huge bolt, which landed four inches deep in the woman's skull. Pieces of her brain were destroyed during the impact and more brain substance was lost when physicians took the bolt out of her head. The woman recovered and lived another forty-two years—without suffering even a headache from her ordeal.

   According to the 1888 edition of *The Medical Press of Western New York*, about one fourth of a man's skull was destroyed when he was caught between a bridge timber and the superstructure of the ship he was working on. The sharp corner of the timber clipped off part of the deckhand's head. Doctors who closed the wound found that the man had lost a substantial amount of brain matter, as well as blood. But as soon as the victim regained consciousness, he talked and dressed himself as though he felt perfectly fine. Except for a few dizzy spells, he was healthy despite the loss of part of his brain, until twenty-six years later when a partial paralysis and unsteady gait developed.

For twenty-seven days, a baby born at St. Vincent's Hospital in New York City in 1935 appeared to be a typical infant—it cried, ate, and moved. Only after its death did doctors discover during the autopsy that it had no brain at all.

In a report prepared by Dr. Jan W. Bruell and Dr. George W. Albee that was delivered to the American Psychological Association in 1957, the physicians noted that they had been forced to perform drastic surgery on a thirty-nine-year-old man. Although they removed the entire right half of the man's brain, the patient survived. And, the doctors concluded, the operation inexplicably "left his intellectual capacity virtually unimpaired."

Dr. Augustin Iturricha and Dr. Nicholas Ortiz of Brazil have documented another baffling brain story. In an address he presented before the Anthropological Society at Sucre, Bolivia, in 1940, Iturricha told of a fourteen-year-old patient with an excruciating headache who was believed to have an abscess of the brain. On autopsy, it was found that the boy's brain mass was virtually detached from the bulb—a condition with medical consequences similar to decapitation. Yet the youngster possessed all his faculties up to the time of his death.

An even stranger case was recounted by the German brain expert Hufeland. When he autopsied a paralyzed man who had been fully rational until the moment of his demise, he found no brain at all—just eleven ounces of water.

Florida UFO

Some of the most spectacular UFO photos ever to emerge were published in Florida's *Gulf Breeze Sentinel* in 1987. The pictures, taken by a local businessman, portrayed a squat, portholed, teapot-shaped UFO. According to the photographer, who asked that his name not be published, a blue beam of light coming from the craft lifted him three feet in the air as he took the photos.

Though the story seemed incredible, it soon turned out that the first photographer was not alone. About a month after the publication of the pictures, another group of similar photos turned up in the *Sentinel* night drop. They were taken by an anonymous reader corroborating the account. What's more, over the days and weeks that followed, more than a hundred *Sentinel* readers wrote in to say that they had seen the strange UFO as well.

Walt Andrus, director of the Mutual UFO Network in Seguin, Texas, eventually heard of the case. Deciding to evaluate it, he went to Gulf Breeze himself. "I had been expecting some kind of hoax, but I don't know what to think now," Andrus says. "These pictures are the best I've seen in more than thirty years of investigation."

Laser physicist Bruce Maccabbee of Silver Spring, Maryland, agrees. "If it's a hoax," he says, "it's just about the most sophisticated one I've ever seen."

THE PRIEST OF BEL

In March of 1892, University of Pennsylvania professor of Assyriology Herman Hilprecht was putting the finishing touches on his master work, a survey of ancient Babylonian inscriptions. But two items—fragments of agate that Hilprecht believed were rings from the Temple of Bel at Nippur—defied identification. Tired and frustrated, the Assyriologist assigned the two pieces to his "unclassified" category and reluctantly put the finishing touches on his book.

That night, Hilprecht dreamed that a tall figure dressed in priestly Babylonian garb took the scholar to the treasure chamber of what Hilprecht immediately recognized as the Temple of Bel. The figure then proceeded to explain that Hilprecht's two puzzling pieces of agate were, in fact, two portions of the same ring and, due to a shortage of agate, it had been divided to form earrings for a statue of the god Ninib. If the two pieces were put together, the dream's priest said, they would reveal the entire inscription Hilprecht had labored to decipher.

The next morning, excited by his dream, Hilprecht immediately examined the agate fragments. Sure enough, the two pieces placed side by side read: "To the god Ninib, son of Bel, his lord, has Kurigalzu, High Priest of Bel, presented this."

THE EARLIEST HUMAN BEINGS?

Mankind has been roaming the earth for only one or two million years, according to accepted paleontological theory. But if some of the fossils discovered in North America are any indication, human beings—or something very humanlike—have been around for hundreds of millions of years.

One amazing discovery was made in the Cumberland Mountains in Jackson County, Kentucky, in the 1880s. As it crossed Big Hill, a wagon train proceeded to break up the sandstone on the peak's summit. When the debris was cleared away, a layer of rock was uncovered and later determined to be more than 300 million years old. Embedded in the ancient rock, excavators found various animal tracks as well as two human footprints, described as being "good sized, toes well spread, and very distinctly marked."

Even earlier, another strange set of footprints was unearthed on the west bank of the Mississippi River at St. Louis in 1816. The prints were ten and a half inches long and four inches wide at the toes. According to Henry Schoolcraft, who examined them, the footprints seemed to have been made by someone used to walking great distances without the benefit of footwear. Schoolcraft described them as being "strikingly natural, exhibiting every muscular impression and swell of the heel and toes, with a precision and faithfulness to nature, which I have not been able to copy." However confident he was that the footprints were genuine, Schoolcraft was nonetheless unable to explain how they managed to appear in a layer of limestone that had hardened 270 million years earlier.

CURE BY LIGHTNING

Samuel Leffers woke one morning in the summer of 1806 with an unusual numbness on his left side. At first, he wasn't alarmed, assuming that he had lain too long on the one side. He soon realized, though, that he also had difficulty speaking and was unable to close his left eye. Although the condition abated somewhat, it seemed to center thereafter in his eye, which remained permanently opened.

Later that summer, according to an account in the *American Journal of Science,* Leffers experienced another misfortune, or so he thought, when he was struck by lightning and knocked unconscious. When he regained consciousness, however, he had also regained use of his limbs. The following day, he noticed that his eyesight had improved and he could soon move the lid. There was only one setback: the electrical shock had impaired his hearing.

NAPOLEON'S DOUBLE

While still the powerful emperor of France, Napoleon Bonaparte sent his representatives all over Europe looking for men who could pass as his double. Four stand-ins were found. One was murdered shortly before Waterloo and another suffered an injury that left him useless as a Napoleon look-alike. But two other men, who looked virtually like the emperor's twin brothers, remained attached to Napoleon's staff for the rest of his reign. One of those doubles, François Eugène Robeaud, may have played the role of Napoleon until his death.

After his defeat at Waterloo, Napoleon was at the mercy of his conquerors. The British decided he must be imprisoned where he could never escape, on the isle of St. Helena. Meanwhile François Robeaud returned home to Baleycourt to be a farmer.

According to historical accounts, Napoleon lived in exile off the coast of Africa until his death. But a series of coincidences suggests that he may have escaped and substituted a double in his place.

In 1818, something unusual happened in Baleycourt. A fine coach pulled up at the home of Napoleon's double, Robeaud. Could the visit have had anything to do with the return to France of General Gourgard, who had just been replaced at the command post at St. Helena? Gourgard's friends were known to include wealthy supporters of Napoleon.

Robeaud told his neighbors that the man in the coach was only a man who wanted to buy some rabbits. But soon Robeaud and his sister disappeared.

Authorities trying to track down the Napoleon double finally located his sister, several years later, living in unexplained luxury in Tours. But where was her brother? She told the inspector assigned to the case, "He went away on a long voyage."

Coincidentally, a stranger named Revard settled in Verona, Italy, in 1818, just after Robeaud disappeared. Along with a business partner named Petrucci, "Revard" opened a small shop. The proprietor looked so much like Napoleon that he was quickly nicknamed "The Emperor."

Meanwhile, on St. Helena, the prisoner known as the real Napoleon was becoming forgetful. His handwriting changed. He was uncouth. French authorities chalked all this up to changes "brought on no doubt by his imprisonment."

On May 5, 1821, Napoleon died in exile. Or did he?

Two years later, the Italian shopkeeper who bore such a striking resemblance to Napoleon abruptly deserted his business and never returned to Verona. Twelve nights after "Revard" disappeared, on September 4, 1823, an intruder was killed as he ran toward an Austrian castle in Schönbrunn, where Napoleon Bonaparte's son lay near death from scarlet fever.

When authorities saw the dead body, they placed the building under guard. Napoleon's wife insisted the body be buried at the castle. The mysterious, unnamed "intruder" was buried in a grave on a direct line with the plots where Napoleon's wife and son were eventually laid to rest.

Thirty years later, the man who had been in business in Verona with the mysterious Napoleon look-alike confessed that he had been paid 100,000 gold crowns for his silence about the true identity of his fellow shopkeeper. He was positive, Petrucci said, that "Revard" was none other than Napoleon Bonaparte himself.

THE GAZELLE BOY OF THE SPANISH SAHARA

In 1970, French anthropologist Jean-Claude Armen discovered a wild child living among a herd of gazelles in the Spanish Sahara. The dark-haired, approximately ten-year-old boy galloped in gigantic bounds with the best of the species, and he seemed perfectly adapted to his environment, living among the gazelles as if he were one of them. Although the boy was never captured, Armen was convinced that he couldn't have been retarded, believing that a retarded child could not be nearly as successful in the wild as was the Gazelle Boy.

BLOODSCOPE READINGS

According to psychologist Takeji Furukawa, in his book *Blood Groups and Temperature,* a person's blood type can reveal a great deal of information. People with type O blood, for example, are the best employees; type B's are freedom-loving people; and type A's are more successful when they're in structured environments. Although published during the thirties and dismissed by medical authorities, the book became the impetus for a national Japanese craze fifty years later.

During the eighties, the Japanese Red Cross began reporting an unprecedented flow of 16 to 19-year-old students to their blood drives. The teenagers responded not only because they felt it was their civic duty but also because they wanted to learn their blood types. Then, consulting Furukawa's book, they could determine their traits accordingly. Blood-based horoscopes even made their way into Japanese women's magazines. A matchmaking service, moreover, began requesting blood type on prospective clients' applications. And a Japanese polling institute indicated blood types among its demographic data. Medical authorities' resumed debunking of *Blood Groups and Temperature* has had little effect on the popularity of bloodscopes.

THE RIDDLE OF THE SPHINX

The Pharaoh Khufu (Chephren in Greek) is said to have built the legendary half-man, half-lion monument known as the Sphinx at Giza around 2700 B.C. But if the theory of Egyptologist Anthony West, author of *The Travelers Key to Ancient Egypt,* is correct, the Sphinx was actually constructed much earlier. And if so, then it follows that the Egyptian civilization is also much older than previously believed.

West points out that the erosion suffered by the stone Sphinx is much worse than its supposed contemporaries, the Pyramids. And the two-foot-deep channels splicing its walls, he says, were cut by water from the Great Floods of Egypt that ravaged the region from 15,000 to 10,000 B.C. If the Sphinx at Giza was, in fact, built before the floods, that would explain why Egyptian culture blossomed so rapidly afterward: its foundation had already been laid and somehow survived the devastating waters.

CLIMBING FISH

In perhaps some kind of arrested evolution, the *Periophthalmus schlosseri,* a fish native to Malaysia, often leaves it aquatic environment to climb trees. When the tide is out the fish squirm around in the mud and wriggle up nearby trees in search of insects. With uncanny agility, they propel themselves by means of two leglike fins.

THE WORLD'S LARGEST TIME CAPSULE

It has been the custom to bury time capsules containing articles of contemporary life and prior epochs in certain World's Fair cities, such as New York, Chicago, and others. But the greatest time capsule of all is not buried; it is over forty-five stories high. The Great Pyramids of Egypt, reputedly the tombs of the Pharaohs Khufu and Khafra of the Fourth Dynasty, have finally been recognized as compendiums of ancient knowledge, geography, astronomy, and science.

Egyptian legends have implied that the purpose of the two greatest pyramids was not so much to function as tombs but to store knowledge (the pyramid of Khufu) and hidden treasure (that of Khafra). During the Middle Ages, the Arab rulers of Egypt had tried mining both pyramids. They were unsuccessful except for removing the smooth limestone facing blocks covered with hieroglyphics from the Great Pyramid and using them, face reversed (and therefore unreadable), for building the Mosque of Ibn Tulum in Cairo.

When Napoleon invaded Egypt in 1798 and defeated the Egyptian armies he ordered his surveyors to use the Great Pyramid as a basis for triangulation for military mapping. To the surprise of the French surveyors they found that a continuation of the diagonal lines crossing the base would neatly enclose the Nile Delta and that the longitudinal meridian would pass through the apex of the pyramid and cut the delta into two equal parts.

French scientists who followed the surveyors discovered a series of remarkable coincidences. For example, they measured the total distance around the base divided by twice its height (taking into account the original height, before some of the great apex stones were removed) and found 3.1416—the exact pi—not the later Greek approximation of 3.1428.

Scientists have since calculated that a straight line due north from the intersection of traverse lines at the base would miss the North Pole by a little over 4 minutes, but since the time when the pyramid was built the North Pole itself has shifted the same amount of time distance. They found that a shaft from the King's Chamber of the pyramid pointed directly to the polestar, then in the Dragon constellation but now in the Big Dipper.

Each side of the pyramid gives, in Egyptian cubits, the number of days in the year as 365, subject to recalculation every 1,460 years. The original height of the pyramid times one billion gives the approximate median distance of the earth to the sun.

When the French, before going to Egypt, had adopted the meter measurement as one ten-thousandth part of a meridian they did not know that the meter was similar to, but not exactly, the length of a pyramidal cubit, indicating one ten-millionth of the polar axis, making the ancient Egyptian measure basically more correct because the meridians vary according to the earth's surface.

Perhaps the most striking figure of all, demonstrating a culture reaching into the very distant past, is suggested by adding the diagonal lines at the base of the pyramid, in pyramid inches giving a figure of 25,826.6 which, coincidentally, represents almost exactly the number of years that the earth's polar axis takes to attain its original position in regard to the sun as it travels through space—25,827 years.

These are only some of the coincidences that suggest that the pyramid of Khufu is not a tomb but rather a time capsule, made of stone, retelling ancient knowledge lost for thousands of years but ever more readable as scientific knowledge catches up to that which was once known in the distant past.

THE GLOUCESTER MONSTER

One of the most well documented sightings of a sea monster occurred in Gloucester Harbor, Massachusetts, in August 1817. So many people witnessed the giant marine creature that a special committee of the Linnaean Society of New England was established to gather sworn affidavits.

A ship's carpenter, Matthew Gaffney, for example, reported that he was on board a boat in the harbor around four-thirty on August 14 when the sea serpent rose from the water not thirty feet away from the vessel. Its head, he said, was as large as a four-gallon keg, his body the width of a barrel, and its length judged to be about forty feet. The creature seemed to approach the boat as if it was going to attack, but then suddenly dived beneath the water. It reappeared a hundred feet away soon after, moving at an estimated rate of one mile per two or three minutes.

A Psychokinetic Adolescent

Bizarre occurrences began taking place in the Ohio household of the Resch family on March 3, 1984. Lights switched on and off without apparent cause. Electrical appliances turned themselves on. The television made mysterious noises even though it was turned off and the screen was blank. The shower began running while no one was in the bathroom. Through it all, there was one common thread: fourteen-year-old Tina Resch, who always seemed to be near the action although not physically responsible for it.

During the next few weeks, Tina made candlesticks dance and hanging lamps swing with frightening regularity. Soon, the entire neighborhood was aware of the phenomenon and family friends and relatives also witnessed objects flying around the house. It wasn't long before researchers and reporters descended in waves upon the frazzled Resches. Two religious groups even attempted an exorcism.

A television news videotape, however, stirred up even more controversy. When the tape, clearly showing Tina levitating a lamp, was played in slow motion, some observers said they saw Tina holding the lamp's cord in her hand. Cries of fraud rose throughout the psychical research community. But others, like *Columbus Dispatch* photographer Fred Shannon, insisted that what was happening was no hoax. Shannon, who expressed his concern for Tina's safety, recounted an incident in which the living room couch moved eighteen inches from the wall and "attacked" Tina, who was sitting in a nearby chair. He also observed the phone move through the air on at least seven occasions, several times hitting Tina so hard she screamed.

Hoping to resolve the situation and the controversy, Tina's parents agreed to have Tina tested at a laboratory near Chapel Hill, North Carolina. During a remarkable series of experiments, Tina was asked to alter the nerve cell firing patterns of giant sea slugs, using nothing more than her mind to accomplish the feat. According to biomedical engineer and neuroscientist Steve Baumann, the tests were successful. Although the sea slug's nerve cells emit a signal every second or two, the scientists didn't pick up a single signal for an interval of twenty-three seconds, during the time Tina's mind was controlling the slugs.

Of course, skeptics are still unconvinced, insisting there will be no proof of Tina's psychokinetic powers until the test results are replicated.

PREMONITION INSURANCE

When Jaime Castell, a Spanish hotel executive, woke from an eerie dream, he thought better than to wake his six-months pregnant wife to tell her about it. There was no need to concern her with the knowledge imparted to him. The voice in the dream, after all, had specifically mentioned the child she was carrying, saying that Castell would not live to see it. Concerned by the portentous dream, Castell followed up the next morning by taking out a life insurance policy for more than $100,000 payable to his wife immediately upon his death.

A few weeks later, Castell was routinely driving home from work when he saw a car traveling from the opposite direction and at more than a hundred miles per hour. As Castell watched in horror, the speeding vehicle careened off the road, across the metal safety bar dividing the highway's lanes and flipped end over end into the air. It was the last thing Castell saw before the car landed on top of his own car. Both drivers were killed instantly.

Often an insurance company will rule an insurance policy invalid if it appears it was purchased with the knowledge that the holder knew he was about to die. Due to the freakish nature of Castell's accident, however, the company couldn't dispute the claim filed later and immediately paid Castell's wife as beneficiary.

THE NEW JERSEY BIGFOOT

In May 1977 several of a New Jersey family's pet rabbits were squeezed to death by something that had clawed at boards and ripped open the wooden barn door to get at the animals during the night. The culprit showed up again the following night, appearing in the now brightly lighted yard. Big and hairy, it looked like a human with a beard and mustache, but had large, glowing red eyes. It swatted at a dog that leaped at it, flinging it twenty feet away.

On the third night, Mr. Sites and three others sat in wait with loaded shotguns. When the creature appeared, they fired at it several times. It growled and ran off into the woods. They were sure they'd hit their target, but they could find no traces of blood afterward.

Investigators from the Society for the Investigation of the Unexplained searched the area, but they never saw the creature, although they heard what they were told was its screaming. Following their examination, the creature was seen several more times, once by the Sites children who saw it crawling through the grass. Its arm was outstretched as though it were injured and seeking help.

MUSICAL ASPIRIN

The woman heard music, songs from the thirties and forties, playing all day long in her head. In frustration, she sought the help of James Allen of the Minneapolis Clinic of Neurology.

Allen investigated every conceivable possibility: Were the woman's neighbors, perhaps, playing their music too loudly? Was her hearing aid malfunctioning and somehow picking up a local radio station? No. Even when the woman was placed in a soundproof room, she still heard the songs.

Allen then undertook a thorough physical examination: the woman was mentally sound, with normal brain wave patterns. With the exception of limited hearing and rheumatoid arthritis, she was otherwise healthy.

The cause of the melodies was, in fact, the twelve aspirin per day taken for her arthritis, Allen finally realized, aware that the drug sometimes causes a ringing in the ears. Because the memory for music is stored in the auditory center of the brain's temporal lobe, the combination of the woman's hearing loss and her heavy use of aspirin stirred her musical memories and brought them into her consciousness. When her aspirin intake was reduced by 50 percent, the sounds gradually subsided, Allen reported in the *New England Journal of Medicine*.

DREAM MURDERS

Baffled police in Oak Park, Illinois, urged area residents to come forward with information regarding the murder of a twenty-four-year-old nursing student on October 4, 1980. A morally upright young man, Steven Linscott felt compelled to tell investigators about the bizarre dreams he had that night between 1:00 and 3:00 A.M. while sleeping next to his wife.

In the dreams, according to the twenty-seven-year-old Bible student and counselor at the Good News Mission, he had seen a man and a woman engaged in what seemed to be a friendly conversation in her home. Suddenly, the man's mood changed and, with a malicious grin, he grabbed a long, heavy metal object and bludgeoned the woman to death. What particularly intrigued Linscott, however, was that the woman had not protested at all during the entire dream beating.

Police were stunned by the amazing similarity between Linscott's dream revelation and the details of the actual homicide. The woman had been bludgeoned by a heavy metal object and had been struck numerous times. The student of yoga, moreover, had been found with her fingers in a Kriya Yoga gesture signifying the acceptance of death. Added to the coincidence, Linscott had, on one occasion at the police station, worn a shirt resembling the one worn by the man in his dream. Concluding that these details could only have been known by the murderer, the police arrested Linscott. Two years later, Linscott was convicted and sentenced to forty years in jail.

In 1984, however, Linscott's conviction was overturned

by two of three judges who heard Linscott's appeal, ruling that the dream could not be considered a confession. The evidence merely raised the possibility of guilt. Enough inconsistencies, moreover, existed between the dream and the actual murder, including the race of the victim. Although the third judge believed that Linscott was guilty, the majority held that the evidence "was plainly not sufficient to exclude every reasonable theory of innocence."

THE LOCH MORAR MONSTER

Loch Ness isn't the only Scottish lake that boasts the habitation of a mysterious marine monster. Sightings at Loch Morar, in fact, go back to 1887, although it wasn't until 1969, that the Loch Morar monster was dubbed Morag.

Duncan MacDonnell and William Simpson were on the lake in their cruiser on the afternoon of August 19, 1969. After a day of fishing, they were heading home when they heard a splash. When they looked out, they saw the Morar monster coming directly at them. When it grazed the side of the boat, it seemed to slow down almost to a full stop, as if running into the vessel was unintentional.

Morag, they reported, was huge, about twenty-five to thirty feet long, with a snakelike head about a foot wide. It had a rough-textured, brown skin and on its back three bumps raised about eighteen inches above the waterline.

But for several minutes, the two men tried to prevent the creature from capsizing the boat. One of the men grabbed a gun and shot at the beast, which then slowly sank and allowed the men to escape.

THE LAKE MONSTER OF BRITISH COLUMBIA

Since the year 1700, there have been about two hundred reports of a huge aquatic animal sighted in Okanagan Lake in British Columbia, Canada. Popularly known as Ogopogo, the creature was observed in 1949, for example, at close range by several people. Leslie Kerry was out on his boat with a vacationing Montreal family when they spotted a large, snakelike form, undulating vertically, alternating between the surface and below it. It appeared to be about thirty feet long and a foot thick and had a forked tail. Meanwhile, on shore, Kerry's wife noticed the form as well, and called her neighbors to take a look. Watching it through binoculars, they described it as smooth and black, with "undulations or coils." They also thought there might have been two creatures, based on the distance between some of the coils.

THE TRAVELING PROPHET AND THE GLASGOW EARTHQUAKE

Edward Pearson, a self-proclaimed "unemployed prophet" from Wales, awoke one morning in late November 1974 with a horrible premonition. Earthquakes in the British Isles, he knew, were as common as snow in July. Even so, Pearson had the impression that the Scottish city of Glasgow would soon be wracked by a substantial tremor.

Seeing no alternative, he believed he must warn Glasgow's citizens of the imminent quake. Although he lacked the necessary funds to travel to Glasgow, the Welshman boarded a train at Inverness without a ticket on December 4, certain that the importance of his visit would convince the train's ticketmaster to make an exception.

Unfortunately for Pearson, the train authorities weren't as understanding as he had expected and his passage was denied. His story was reported the following day in the Dundee, Scotland, *Courier and Advertiser*, with a somewhat tongue-in-cheek bias. Three weeks later, however, when an earthquake rattled Glasgow, destroying numerous buildings in the city and surrounding area, the newspapermen realized they had scoffed at a most accurate prediction.

AUTO COINCIDENCE

When Thomas Baker came out of a shopping center in Sheboygan, Wisconsin, his first thought was that his car had been stolen. But after a few minutes of searching, he saw the maroon American Motors Concord not far from where he had originally parked it. He unlocked the door and slid inside, but was baffled when his six-foot-six-inch body didn't fit comfortably between the seat and the steering wheel. And when he looked around him, he noticed many unfamiliar objects in place of what should have been there. Confused, and unsure of what else to do, Baker called the police.

While Baker was later explaining the puzzling situation to the patrolman who responded to his call, an elderly couple pulled up in an identical 1978 maroon Concord. They, too, had been mystified when they realized there were unfamiliar items in the car they had thought was their own. A subsequent check of license plates proved that Baker and the elderly couple had, indeed, confused their cars.

According to American Motors, the real coincidence lay in the fact that each owner's key opened the other's car door, something that had a one-in-a-thousand chance of occurring. But when you consider the matching color and model, as well as the fact that the cars were parked in the same place at the same time, the odds become more like ten thousand to one.

In an even more bizarre twist, however, Baker and the elderly couple had the same last name.

THE CURSED KIMONO

In the annals of legendary cursed clothing, perhaps none created nearly as much furor and destruction as that attributed to a mid-seventeenth-century Japanese kimono. Three young women each successively owned the garment and all three died before they ever had a chance to wear it. Believing the kimono was evil and the cause of the girls' deaths, a Japanese priest declared that it would be cremated in February 1657. But as the kimono was set ablaze, a sudden and violent wind blew up and fanned the flames until they were out of control. The ensuing fire destroyed three-quarters of Tokyo and killed 100,000 people.

BISMARCK, JEFFERSON, AND THE NUMBER 3

They may have lived during different periods and in different countries, but Thomas Jefferson and Prince Bismarck had at least one thing in common: the number 3 figured greatly in their lives. Among other tertiary facts, the third president of the United States, Thomas Jefferson, was his parents' third son and the family's third Thomas. He wrote the Declaration of Independence at the age of thirty-three, for three years served as the third ambassador to France, was appointed the third president of the American Philosophical Society, and lost the presidential election in 1796 by three votes.

A passionate lover of the three arts—Architecture, Painting, and Music—Jefferson hated three things: royalty, nobility, and fanaticism. Jefferson would probably, then, have been displeased by Bismarck's three titles: count, duke, and prince. Like Jefferson, however, Bismarck studied in three schools, although the prince then went on to serve three kings, fight in three wars, have three horses killed under him, sign three peace treaties, serve as ambassador to three countries, and establish the Triple Alliance. And unlike Jefferson, Bismarck, the father of three children, escaped three attempts on his life. His coat of arms, moreover, bore three intertwining oak leaf sprigs.

FOOTWEAR 280 MILLION YEARS AGO?

William Meister, along with his wife and two daughters, was on a rock and fossil hunting expedition in Antelope Spring, near Delta, Utah. Amateur fossil buffs, the Meisters had already unearthed the remains of several trilobites—small marine invertebrates that had become extinct 280 million years ago but had been the forerunners of crabs and shrimp. From the same rock strata, Meister pulled out a two-inch-thick slab. Splitting it, he was surprised to find what seemed to be a fossilized footprint. If that wasn't unusual enough, the foot had apparently been wearing a sandal and had crushed a trilobite beneath it.

If Meister's fossil evidence meant what it seemed to indicate, Meister reasoned that paleontologists must be wrong on at least one of two arguments. Either trilobites, known to have thrived for more than 320 million years, had not become extinct 280 million years ago; or contrary to theory, humanoids were around much earlier than the 2-million-year date paleontologists have set for their appearance. The footwear threw another kink into modern theories: Historians project that sandals, shoes, and other footwear have been worn for only several thousand years.

Meister attempted to have his find examined by local university geologists, but they weren't interested: Meister was simply wrong in the assumptions he had made about the find. So he finally went to the press with his discovery. Still, the academic community was uninterested. James Madsen, curator of the Museum of Earth Science at the University of Utah, for one, flatly refuted Meister's claim that he had evidence of humanoids existing at the time of the trilobites. "There were no men 600 million years ago," he stated. "Neither were there monkeys or bears or ground sloths to make pseudohuman tracks. What man-thing could possibly have been walking around on this planet before vertebrates even evolved?"

What indeed? Some people familiar with this case speculate that, perhaps long before the appearance of *Homo sapiens*, some shoe-wearing biped from another world may have walked upon the earth.

TOP SECRET PUZZLE

The absolute secrecy surrounding the Allies' plan to invade Europe during World War II made it necessary to devise an elaborate system of code words to alert agents to intended actions. Called Operation Overlord, the invasion plan included distinct phases, each with its own code name. The naval initiative, for example, was known as Neptune. The French destination and rendezvous points were known as Omaha and Utah, and an artificial harbor, Mulberry, was where the arsenal and supplies were to be stationed. But thirty-three days before the scheduled invasion date, many of the code words curiously appeared in the crossword puzzle of London's *Daily Telegraph*. Then, only four days before the plan was in operation, the word *overlord* showed up in the crossword puzzle.

Concerned that a Nazi spy had gotten hold of the code and was publicizing Operation Overlord through the crossword puzzle, security agents stormed the *Daily Telegraph* offices. To their surprise, they found only a bewildered schoolteacher named Leonard Dawes who had been composing the *Daily Telegraph* puzzle for twenty years. Dawes finally managed to convince the agents that the appearance of the key code word in the crossword puzzle was just a coincidence.

THE STAR OF NINE MOONS

Living among the Efe pygmies of the isolated Ituri forest of central Africa in 1957 and 1958, French anthropologist Jean Pierre Hallet learned that the Efe referred to the planet Saturn as "the star of nine moons." The fact about Saturn's moons, of course, wasn't a surprise. Astronomers had known about the moons since 1899, when the ninth was discovered. An unsuspected tenth moon was observed by the Voyager space probe when it orbited the planet in 1980. Even so, no one has any idea how the Efes knew about even nine moons, since none of the moons can be seen with the naked eye, and the pygmics' lack of technical development certainly precluded even an awareness of the telescope.

THE PRESERVED BODY OF
ST. BERNADETTE

In 1858, Bernadette Soubirous, then a fourteen-year-old French girl, saw visions of the Virgin Mary at a spring in Lourdes, France, now one of the most famous Catholic shrines. Bernadette later became a nun in the order of the Sisters of Notre-Dame of Nevers and died at the age of thirty-five. For forty-five years following her death, however, Bernadette's body was exhumed three times to determine the condition of her corpse, its possible incorruptibility being a sign of sainthood, according to Catholic Church tradition. Although there had been some decomposition as a result of the examinations, investigators found, Bernadette's body remained remarkably preserved. Today, it is on permanent display in the chapel of the Convent of St. Gildard in France.

OCEAN OASIS

Captain Neal Curry, his wife and two children, and a crew of thirty-two set sail in Curry's ship *Lara* from Liverpool, England, in 1881. On their way to San Francisco, a violent fire broke out on board and they were forced to abandon the vessel off the western coast of Mexico. The three lifeboats drifted aimlessly through the Pacific Ocean, with no land or other ships in sight. Soon, debilitating thirst and hunger overwhelmed the passengers and before long seven people had lapsed into unconsciousness.

While asleep one night, Curry dreamed that the water changed color from blue to green. He tasted it and found that it was fresh and drinkable. When he groggily struggled awake, weaker than he ever thought possible, Curry was astonished to see the water surrounding the cluster of lifeboats was indeed green. And just as he'd foreseen in his dream, he mustered enough strength to lower a container into the ocean. Lifting it, he raised the water to his lips. Sure enough, the water was fresh—and drinkable.

Having been in the lifeboats for twenty-three days after abandoning their burning ship, Captain Curry, his family, and crew landed on the Mexican coast. Because of the mysterious freshwater oasis they'd accidentally discovered in the middle of the ocean, all thirty-six lives had been saved.

THE HEALING POWERS OF PADRE PIO

The spontaneous appearance of stigmata, the replication of the wounds Jesus Christ suffered on the cross, on a seemingly normal person is considered a holy occurrence in the Catholic faith. A most remarkable case of such stigmata was reported in the Italian town of Loggia in the early part of this century. A Capuchin monk known as Padre Pio not only was marked by the nail wounds in his hands and feet and that of the sword that pierced his side, but he was also able to heal the sick and injured by simply laying his hands on their bodies. On one such occasion, a nine-year-old boy, so hunchbacked that he could only crawl through the streets, was suddenly able to stand up straight after one touch of the monk's bleeding hand.

Padre Pio, born in 1887, first felt the pain in his feet, hands, and side when he was twenty-eight years old, but doctors were unable to determine the cause. Three years later, he was praying at the altar when he collapsed in pain. Fellow monks found him unconscious some time later, bleeding from sites in his hands, feet, and side with no apparent cause. The monks immediately realized he displayed the stigmata of Christ.

While Padre Pio was revered and respected throughout Italy and later the world, he still encountered skeptics and critics. One of them, a Dr. Ricciardi, who lived in the town of San Giovanni Rotondo, not far from the Capuchin monastery, was stricken with a brain tumor in 1929. Wanting to die in peace, he refused to admit Padre Pio into his bedroom. But death did not come easily to Dr. Ricciardi, and when Padre Pio unexpectedly appeared at the physician's bedside, he was willing to accept the administration of the monk's healing power. By the end of that year, Dr. Ricciardi was fully recovered.

BLUE-SKINNED PEOPLE

Blue-skinned people are an oddity of nature, but in most cases they can be biologically explained. Some natives of the Ozarks, for example, have a pastel blue hue due to genetic abnormalities caused by decades of interbreeding. Several known diseases can also cause a bluish discoloration of the skin. But high in the Chilean Andes, a group of true blue-skinned people were discovered at an altitude of twenty-five hundred feet, higher than human beings were thought capable of surviving over prolonged periods.

Mountaineer and physiologist John West of the University of California at San Diego's School of Medicine discovered the small group of miners whose skin has evidently turned blue to adapt to the lack of oxygen at nearly twenty thousand feet above sea level. The miners apparently produce large amounts of hemoglobin, the oxygen-carrying pigment in human red blood cells. The excess hemoglobin shows through the skin, giving it its bluish tint. The men have probably increased the depth and rate of their breathing. And because they were born and raised at high altitudes, they already have a head start in their adaptation.

Tibetan priests, of course, also spend a great deal of time at equally high altitudes, but the miners in the Andes do it while performing strenuous work.

THE LAWYER WHO PRESENTED HIS CASE TOO WELL

Thomas McGean was a local troublemaker who, in 1871, was accused of shooting and killing a man in a barroom brawl. His defense attorney, Clement Vallandigham, contended that the victim had shot himself as he attempted to draw his gun from his pocket while trying to rise from a kneeling position. One evening, Vallandigham was meeting with fellow defense lawyers and demonstrated how the scenario occurred.

Earlier, the attorney had placed two pistols on the bureau, one empty and one loaded. Grabbing the loaded one by mistake, Vallandigham put it in his pant's pocket and cocked it. He reenacted the scene as he imagined it occurred. But when he pulled the trigger, he shot himself, exactly as he'd argued the dead man had. Vallandigham died twelve hours later. This convincing reenactment resulted in the subsequent acquittal of McGean.

THE MAN WHO WOULD NOT HANG

Young Will Purvis was tried for the murder of a farmer in Columbia, Mississippi, and although he insisted he was innocent throughout the trial, the twelve jurors found him guilty. After he was sentenced to hang and was leaving the courtroom, Purvis shouted at the jurors, "I'll live to see the last one of you die."

On February 7, 1894, Purvis stood on the gallows, a heavy noose snugly tied around his neck. But instead of dangling and his neck breaking when the trapdoor opened, Purvis fell right through. The knot on the noose had mysteriously become untied and the noose, therefore, had slipped over the convicted man's head. Officials retied the noose and set up the execution a second time. The crowd gathered at the site was of a different mind, however. To them, Purvis's salvation was a miracle and he was obviously not meant to hang. Screaming, singing, and shouting their praises to God, the onlookers had enough influence to postpone the execution. Several appeals filed by Purvis's attorney were denied and the hanging was rescheduled for December 12, 1895, despite the fact that Purvis was now a popular figure.

A few nights before the second scheduled execution, a small group of admirers broke Purvis out of prison and he went into hiding to await the inauguration of a new governor sympathetic to his plight. In 1896, however, he surrendered and his sentence was commuted to life imprisonment.

By 1898, the outpouring of letters and favorable public

opinion finally had an effect: Purvis was pardoned and released from prison. It wasn't until 1917, however, that he was vindicated. On his deathbed, a man named Joseph Beard confessed to the murder for which Purvis would have been executed.

In a postscript to this curious tale, Purvis died on October 13, 1938, three days after the death of the last surviving juror at his trial. Just as he had promised, Purvis had outlived them all.

BIGGER THAN "JAWS"

Life in our planet's oceans remains a mystery to even the most ardent researchers. In fact, many marine biology experts believe that there are probably countless sea creatures still unidentified. Two sharks captured off the coasts of Hawaii and California, for example, may be one such specimen—a shark species thought to have been extinct for millions of years. The two fifteen-foot-long monsters, dubbed megamouths because of their scooplike jaws, are tantalizing evidence that there are many more unknown animals where these two came from.

International Society of Cryptozoology's Richard Greenwell cites eyewitness accounts from around the world attesting to the existence of abnormally large sharks. Author Zane Grey, for example, reported seeing a forty-foot-long yellow and green shark in the South Pacific during the twenties. And in 1977, some fishermen pulled their boat alongside a giant white shark that they estimated to be more than thirty feet long. Besides such unusually long sharks, Greenwell says there's no reason to think that prehistoric sharks, such as the presumably extinct *Carcharodon megalodon*, couldn't still be alive and well deep below the ocean's surface.

BLAZING BEACH

Just after dinner on September 1, 1905, the guests at Kittery Point's Hotel Parkfield on the coast of Maine were enjoying the late summer air when they were startled by an amazing sight: the beach had burst into flames. Both the sand and the surface of the water were spouting fire and thick, sulfurous smoke. A loud crackling sound could be heard up to a hundred yards away, and the flames, rising to a height of one foot, continued to burn for more than forty-five minutes.

One curious guest grabbed a handful of sand, but quickly dropped it when the intense heat scalded his hand. Other guests scooped up some sand in a pot and took it into the hotel where they added water to it. To their surprise, gas bubbles escaped from the sand and, as they broke at the surface of the water, they ignited.

According to one explanation for the bizarre event, a layer of seaweed buried beneath the sand—both on the beach and below the water near the shore—had fermented, creating pockets of flammable gas that reacted with the air in such a way as to cause the fire. That was only one possibility, however, and never proven to be the case.

BURN IMMUNITY

Despite its mystical quality, the phenomenon of firewalking, the ability to cross a bed of hot coals in one's bare feet, can be traced to a simple case of the mind's being trained to control the sensation of pain for a limited period of time. But the amazing abilities of a nineteenth-century Denton, Maryland, blacksmith evidences an actual immunity to intense heat.

Nathan Coker was born in 1814, a slave belonging to a Hillsborough, Maryland, lawyer named Purnell. His owner's mistreatment of the boy included starving him, and it was the constant hunger that prompted the discovery of his unusual gift. One afternoon, when the cook had left the kitchen, Nathan reached into a vat of boiling water, pulled out a cooking dumpling, and popped it into his mouth. He then realized that he had felt no pain, not on his hand or in his mouth. He soon found that he could touch and eat any food, no matter how hot. He'd drink the fat off the top of boiling water and would even down scalding coffee. He claimed, in fact, that it was *cold* liquids and foods that gave him the greatest discomfort. After he was freed, Nathan went to work as a blacksmith, and it was there that his unique ability came in quite handy. As Nathan told it, "I often take my iron out of the forge with my hand when red hot, but it don't burn."

As word of Nathan's gift spread, he was invited to give a demonstration before prominent Easton, Maryland, citizens, including two newspaper editors and two physicians. The feat was even reported in the pages of the *New York Herald* in 1871. According to eyewitnesses, Coker placed an iron shovel, heated until it was white hot, on the soles of his bare feet. After the shovel was reheated, he ran his tongue over it. Lead pellets were also melted into liquid and poured into Coker's hand and the blacksmith then poured the substance into his mouth. As the astonished audience watched, Nathan rolled the molten lead around his teeth and gums until it had solidified.

After each feat, the physicians examined Nathan, but found no indication that his flesh had been affected.

Nineteenth-Century Flying Saucers

A story that appeared in the January 25, 1878, issue of the Denison, Texas, *Daily Herald* may have contained the first known use of the word *saucer* to describe a UFO. The article recounted the experience of John Martin, a farmer living just south of Denison.

On the afternoon of January 24, Martin was working in his fields when he looked up and suddenly saw a dark, disc-shaped object in the clear sky. The object traveled "at a wonderful speed," he told the *Daily Herald* reporter, and went on to report that it "resembled a saucer skimming across the heavens."

THE MYSTERY OF DOWSING

Traditionally, dowsing is the ability to locate underground water, but many practitioners nowadays also seek buried objects. Their instrument is nothing more than a forked stick. Regardless of what dowsers seek, the art has probably been around since prehistoric times, if Algerian rock paintings are any indication. Ancient Egyptians as well as the early Chinese also seem to have dabbled in the art. Written accounts, however, date back only to the Middle Ages.

Although little is known about how it works, speculation falls into two categories: physical and psychical. According to those who practice dowsing, some force emanates from subterranean water or buried objects and is transmitted to the dowsing stick. The force, they believe, may be an energy field, electromagnetism, or even radiation. But this doesn't explain how a swinging pendulum dangled over a map can pinpoint an object's physical buried location.

Map dowsing falls more in line with the psychical explanation. The theory is that the dowser attunes his or her mind to a universal consciousness providing information that causes the dowser's muscles to involuntarily react. Such a reaction then stirs the pendulum to vibrate, indicating the site where the object will be found. Some dowsers, in fact, claim to not even need an instrument; they simply "know" where the object is.

In 1951, when the General Motors (GM) Corporation opened a huge plant in semiarid Port Elizabeth, the South African area was suffering a major drought. The GM plant, like other large factories, required a dependable water supply. Water, of course, usually runs deep within the ground, even when the surface is bone dry, but there were no reliable wells. Scientific searches for the sublevel water had been unsuccessful.

With everything to lose, the desperate GM officials resorted to using a dowser and the unorthodox method of water witching to find water by simply sensing its location beneath the surface. The plant's superintendent called in C. J. Bekker, a local dowser who also happened to be a GM employee and agreed to help.

With his arms folded across his chest, Bekker wandered around the grounds of the GM plant for half an hour. Then, he suddenly stopped and began to shake uncontrollably. GM officials would find fresh water, Bekker said, if they dug exactly where he was standing. The dowser then went on to find two more areas.

Although they marked the sites for future reference, the officials were skeptical. To convince themselves to trust Bekker, they blindfolded him and had him go through the process again. Without being able to see where he was walking, Bekker returned to the same areas he had previously indicated.

The company had to drill in only one of Bekker's locations to find all the water for the huge plant.

ABRAHAM LINCOLN AND THE DANCING PIANO

During the 1860s, even American president Abraham Lincoln was attracted to spiritualism which was at the height of its vogue. At a seance in the home of a Mrs. Laurie and her daughter Mrs. Miller, Lincoln watched

Miller make a piano beat time with heavy thuds on the floor as she played during a trance.

As she began to play, the piano's front legs repeatedly rose from the floor and then dropped to the floor. One guest asked to sit on the piano to verify that it moved, and the medium replied that anyone who wished could sit on it. Four people did: a congressional lobbyist, a judge, and two soldiers accompanying Lincoln. When Mrs. Miller resumed her playing, the piano again began rising, as much as four inches off the floor, and then fell.

AN ORPHAN'S VISIT FROM MOTHER

One night in 1878, the Reverend Charles Jupp, warden of the Orphanage and Convalescent Home at Aberdour, Scotland, gave up his bed to unexpected overnight guests at the orphanage. So he slept with the children in the dormitory, on a cot near three children who had just arrived following their mother's death.

In the middle of the night, jolted out of his sleep for no apparent reason, he surveyed the dark room. Then he noticed a strange but wonderful sight: a small, glowing cloud, in his own words "as bright as the moon on an ordinary moonlit night," hovering over the youngest of the three recently orphaned children as they slept.

Certain he wasn't dreaming, the minister felt he just had to touch the otherworldly apparition. But as he went to rise from the bed, some invisible but benevolent force seemed to keep him from getting up. He heard nothing, but felt and perfectly understood the directive, "Lie down. It won't hurt you." Calmed by the spectral force, he fell back to sleep.

The next morning, he rose at his customary time and, at 6:00 A.M., began dressing the children. When he went to the child who had lain sleeping beneath the spectral cloud, he found the boy unusually silent. Then he looked up at the minister with an extraordinary expression on his face and said, "Mr. Jupp, my mother came to me last night. Did you see her?"

Mr. Jupp didn't answer, but simply smiled and told the boy to get ready for breakfast.

THE MYSTERY OF CAWDOR CASTLE

According to legend, Scotland's Cawdor Castle was the scene of King Duncan's murder by Macbeth in 1040, a tale immortalized by William Shakespeare. But the castle is interesting for another, more unusual reason: on its chimney is a carving representing a fox smoking a tobacco pipe and holding it exactly as a human smoker would. The engraved date on the stone is 1510. But tobacco was introduced into England by Sir Walter Raleigh in 1585, seventy-five years *after* the smoking fox was carved.

FIVE FIERY DAYS IN JANUARY

Mysterious and spontaneous flames plagued the Williamson family for five days in January 1932. During those cold winter days in Bladenboro, North Carolina, their clothing as well as household items suddenly ignited for no apparent reason. Neither the police, utility company officials, nor arson experts were ever able to determine the cause or offer any logical explanation for the phenomenon.

On the first occasion, Mrs. Williamson's dress flared up. Soon after, the family discovered Mr. Williamson's pants ablaze as they hung in the closet. Then a bed, curtains, and other articles went up in flames. In each case, there were bluish, jetlike flames unaccompanied by any smoke or odor. Even more bizarre, nothing else nearby was ever affected.

THE NIGHTMARE OF BEING BURIED ALIVE

The night after Max Hoffman was buried, his mother had a nightmare, envisioning her son trapped inside his dark grave. His hands clenched below his right cheek, the five-year-old boy was tossing and turning as he struggled to escape his prison of death.

Waking from the horrible dream, the mother pleaded with her husband to have the coffin disinterred, but he refused, believing that she was merely refusing to accept the fact that their son was dead. The next night, however, Mrs. Hoffman had the same dream. Her husband finally agreed to appease the emotionally distraught woman.

With a neighbor's assistance, Mr. Hoffman went to the cemetery at one o'clock in the morning, and exhumed his son's body. It lay exactly as Mrs. Hoffman had dreamed, but showed no sign of life. Even so, they took the boy's body to the doctor who had pronounced him dead. Reluctantly, the doctor attempted to revive him. An hour later, they were shocked to see an eyelid twitch.

Within a week, Max had fully recovered and went on to live to be nearly ninety years old.

MATTHEW MANNING'S PERSONAL POLTERGEIST

The house in Cambridge, England, was neither strange nor spooky, and it wasn't old enough to have a history of hauntings. But in February 1967, Derek Manning began noticing that objects were mysteriously moving around.

It started with a silver beer tankard that Manning kept on a wooden shelf. One morning, and for several mornings afterward, the tankard was found on the floor, and Manning's three children denied they were in any way responsible. Sprinkling talcum powder on the shelf around the tankard to try to catch the culprit, Manning was astonished to find the powder undisturbed in the morning, even though the tankard was once again on the floor.

Manning finally called the police who referred him to the Cambridge Psychical Research Society. They suggested that a poltergeist, a mischevious ghost, was the probable cause for the moving objects and that the activity centered around the children, particularly eleven-year-old Matthew. And, in fact, the disturbances ceased when the children were sent to visit relatives for a while. As soon as they returned, however, so did the poltergeist, and this time, even heavy furniture was displaced. The activity continued until Matthew went off to boarding school.

The phenomenon reached its peak when Matthew was

home during the Christmas holidays in 1970. Matthew himself often heard a scratching noise behind his bedroom wall and footsteps outside his window. On one particularly frightening night, the scratching seemed to come from the direction of a cupboard in his room and, when he flicked the light on, he noticed the cupboard had been moved at least eighteen inches from the wall and toward him. He quickly turned the light out and almost simultaneously the bed began to shake violently. Too terrified to move, the boy simply waited for what would happen next. When he felt the lower end of the bed rise, however, Matthew raced from the room and spent the rest of the night in his parents' room. The remainder of the night passed without incident, but in the morning, the family found the house in a shambles.

As if the overturned furniture were not enough, bric-a-brac began flying around. It got to the point where family members would ask for something to be moved and the poltergeist complied. Puddles also appeared on the floors throughout the house and ghostly messages were scrawled in childish handwriting on the walls. One eerie inscription read, "Matthew, beware." With that, Matthew quickly returned to boarding school, but the poltergeist evidently followed him, wreaking the same kind of havoc there as it had in the Manning household.

Finally, Matthew attempted to rechannel the spirit's energies through automatic writing and spontaneous drawings and judging that perhaps 5 percent of the results actually came from entities and not from his own mind. In any event, the disturbances eventually ceased, and Matthew went on to continue his paranormal experiments and developed considerable psychic talents of his own.

THE MAN-BEAST OF
WASHINGTON STATE

Grays Harbor County, Washington, deputy sheriff Verlin Herrington was driving home late one night when he encountered what he first thought was a bear. Proceeding along Deekay Road at approximately 2:35 A.M. on July 26, 1969, he slammed on his brakes and screeched to a halt. Turning his spotlight on the beast, he realized it wasn't a bear. And although it walked upright, it wasn't human either. It was covered with thick, brownish black hair, except on its humanlike face, which had a dark leathery appearance. Instead of paws, it had feet, its toes as well as its fingers quite distinct. And it appeared to be about seven and a half feet tall and must have weighed at least three hundred pounds.

Fearful, Herrington drew his gun, but before he could take a shot at it, the creature strode quickly into the woods and out of sight. The next day, the deputy returned to the site, where he found and photographed a footprint that measured eighteen and a half inches long.

PREHISTORIC SAUNAS

Archaeologists have long thought that the European features known as burnt mounds were nothing more than cooking areas. But that was an assumption based mostly on historical references to the use of hot stones to boil water. That may be true, but the purpose may have not been for cooking as much as for steaming. Recent excavations, in fact, have unearthed evidence to suggest the burnt mounds may actually have been early versions of our modern saunas. According to University of Birmingham professor of European prehistory Lawrence Barfield, the mounds may have been sweathouses or sauna baths: To support his idea, Barfield cites the absence of animal remains which would have been proof that the mounds had been used for cooking, but there are troughs that could have held water for steam.

The evidence, coupled with historical accounts that indicate a prevalence of marijuana use, leads Barfield to speculate that as early as the first millennium B.C., our ancestors may have been purposefully engaging in thought drugs while sitting in the prehistoric equivalent of a hot tub.

THE RAINMAKERS

In the final days of the nineteenth century, an Australian named Frank Melbourne arrived in America advertising himself as a professional rainmaker. He'd set up a canvas wall around a thirty-square-foot area where he would mix his secret formula. Soon the fumes would rise through a thirty-foot-high smokestack and then escape into the atmosphere.

Melbourne's wasn't a new idea, of course. Conditioned to know that rains always followed forest fires, shamans would create great fires in time of drought. Even Civil War soldiers accepted rain as a natural consequence of battle and referred to them as "battle storms." The clouds of cannon smoke that rose into the sky, they knew from experience, were soon followed by rain clouds. Perhaps it was just coincidence, maybe not.

In 1891, Goodland, Kansas, farmers collectively hired Frank Melbourne to break the drought, and when he began his routine, there hadn't been a cloud in sight for days. But then Melbourne's chemically created smoke filled the air and by midafternoon the clouds rolled in thick and dark. That night, the farmers stood in the downpour, rejoicing.

The following year, Melbourne's miracle working was not needed. The rains came in abundance. So the last anyone heard of the Australian rainmaker, he was off to Africa. In his stead, however, there were other rainmakers. C. B. Jewell's spectacular method of producing rain incorporated a bundle of dynamite tied to a small balloon sent five hundred to a thousand feet in the air, where the explosives were detonated via telephone wire. He entertained the public with fireworks and satisfied the farmers who hired him with great downpours.

Perhaps the best-known rainmaker, however, was Charles Mallory Hatfield, who had practically a lifelong interest in rainmaking, conducting his own experiments after reading Edward Powers's 1871 book on the "science of pluviculture," which attracted so much attention even the United States Congress appropriated money in 1891 to investigate Powers's theory that rain could be coaxed out of the sky through scientific methods.

By 1902, Hatfield was a full-time rainmaker, building huge wooden tanks standing on stout legs that held the tanks twelve feet above the ground. He, too, used chemicals, dumping them into the tanks, stirring and mixing them, adding water and a few gallons of acid, tightly covering the tank with a wooden lid. After about twenty minutes, he'd lift the lid and the malodorous vapor would escape into the atmosphere. In twenty-five years, he contracted five hundred rainmaking jobs in the Los Angeles area, ranging in cost from fifty to ten thousand dollars. In one experiment, he agreed to fill the Lake Hemet reservoir, producing eleven inches of rain and raising the reservoir's water level by twenty-two feet. Hatfield's greatest and unequalled success, however, occurred in the Mojave Desert where he produced forty inches of rain in three hours.

THE BARDIN BOOGER MAN

Deep in the pine forests of Bardin, Florida, a big, hairy, manlike beast with a pug nose lurks, waiting to leap out and shake passing cars. Neighborhood residents call him the Bardin Booger, and he's become somewhat of a hometown celebrity. Bud Key, owner of Bud's Grocery in the heart of Bardin, sells T-shirts emblazoned with pictures of the monster. And a local country music performer even wrote a song about the Booger Man.

Size thirteen footprints have been found in the areas where the Booger has been spotted. Eyewitnesses include Doug Crew, a longtime Bardin resident who was sitting with two young women in his truck one evening when the van began to vibrate violently. "The best way I've come to describe it," Crew said afterward, "is like a dog when it shakes water off its back."

While the phenomenon has induced some pranksters to fake Booger prints and rig up sound systems on their vehicles to produce weird sounds, a number of people claim to have seen the Booger. And as Key says, "As far as I'm concerned he's still around."

Out-of-Body Rescue

At sea for weeks, a British ship out of Liverpool, England, was moving through the icy North Atlantic waters and headed toward Nova Scotia in 1828, when first mate Robert Bruce encountered a stranger in the captain's cabin. The man, who Bruce knew wasn't a crew member, was writing on the blackboard. Suspecting the scribbler was a stowaway, Bruce ran to get the captain. When the two men returned to the cabin, the stranger was gone, but he had left a message on the blackboard, reading: "Steer to the Nor'-west."

Calling all hands on deck, the captain had each one write the message, but no one's handwriting matched that of the stranger. Even so, the captain felt it might be wise to follow the mysterious suggestion and ordered the ship's course to be altered.

Not long after the captain ordered the crew to steer to the northwest, the ship's lookout spotted another ship, which appeared to be wedged in the ice of the frigid North Atlantic. When all its passengers were taken aboard the British ship, Bruce spotted a man resembling the scrawler in the captain's cabin. His handwriting was tested and, sure enough, matched that on the blackboard.

According to the icebound ship's passenger, he had fallen asleep just after the vessel had become mired in the ice. When he awoke, he had the certain impression that they would be rescued. Evidently, the man had had an out-of-body experience, projecting himself onto the British ship to deliver an SOS call.

GEOMAGNETISM AND ESP

Based on the often unsuccessful demonstration of ESP abilities in controlled test situations, skeptics have long argued that so-called ESP is nothing more than chance or luck: After all, if the phenomenon were real, there is no reason why a subject should perform well one day and poorly the next. But two separate research groups have shown that changes in the earth's magnetic field might actually be responsible for the inconsistency of the psychic ability. Since it's known that fluctuating geomagnetism affects biological activities, it is reasonable to assume it also influences psi.

In a survey of remote-viewing experiments conducted during a five-year period, Marcia Adams, president of the Time Research Institute of Woodside, California, found a clear correlation between successful tests and geomagnetic fluctuations. In the twenty-four- to forty-eight-hour period before successful tests, the geomagnetic-field measurements were generally low; the exact opposite was true before unsuccessful tests.

The research psychology and neuroscience professor, Michael Persinger, at Canada's Laurentian University, moreover, supports Adams's findings. Persinger chose to look at "crisis apparitions"—those situations in which an individual is able to sense a disturbing occurrence before it actually happens. Going through collected accounts taken from as far back as 1868, he was able to determine a significant connection between such premonitions and periods of low geomagnetic activity.

THE MISSING LAKE

A small lake had nestled in the Italian Dolomites for hundreds of years. In July 1980, however, the calm, peaceful body of water vanished into thin air, leaving nothing but mud and a few fish behind. One minute, people had been fishing and swimming in the lake. The next, a great spiral of water roared up out of the center of the lake, continuing to rise until the lake was completely gone. Hydraulic engineers and geologists have never been able to explain the phenomenon.

LEPENSKI VIR

The west bank of the Danube River in Yugoslavia was not thought to be significant in terms of prehistoric civilizations. It had been assumed that Neolithic Europe had not been the birthplace of any independent civilization, but that its cultural development had been, in large part, determined by Near Eastern influences. But in 1965, archaeologists made an amazing discovery at a horseshoe-shaped bend in the Danube where they found a small, but highly organized settlement that dated to 5800 B.C.

Remarkable as a model of social, economic, religious,

and artistic organization, the prehistoric European settlement, which the archaeologists dubbed Lepenski Vir, seems to have risen independently of any outside influence, unless the builders were travelers or refugees from a far more distant area. In addition to a sanctuary containing stone sculptures of extraordinary sophistication, a central plaza fanned out into streets lined with trapezoidal and other geometrically shaped buildings. The floors of the dwellings, moreover, had been paved with an ingenious mortar of limestone, water, gravel, and sand.

PARANORMAL PHENOMENA AND EXORCISMS

Adolf Rodewyk, the Jesuit priest who wrote *Possessed by Satan,* the 1963 definitive handbook on exorcism, urged priests to rule out all medical explanations for an apparent demonic possession before undertaking the dangerous ritual. He may or may not have followed his own warning before submitting a German student to an unsuccessful exorcism that ended tragically in 1976.

A student at the University of Würzburg in West Germany, Anneliese Michel had been under medical care for epilepsy for four years before she began displaying unprovoked rage, violence, and other abnormal behavior. At the request of the young woman's parents, the local parish priest counseled the girl and, after consulting Rodewyk, then eighty-one years old, recommended exorcism. The ritual soon began under the guiding hands of Reverends Arnold Renz and Ernst Alt.

After several months of harrowing yet fruitless exorcism, however, the twenty-three-year-old woman, now weighing only seventy pounds, died of malnutrition and dehydration on July 1, 1976. Less than two years later, Renz, Alt, and Anneliese's parents were charged with negligent homicide. The priests were eventually convicted, but their six-month prison sentences were suspended. The tragic case led to the German Bishops Conference to rule that no exorcism would take place without the presence of a doctor.

But were Anneliese's demons the successful parties in the exorcism? Or did the young woman die because she wasn't possessed? Some familiar with the circumstances believe the case may actually have been one of multiple personality, a syndrome that manifests two or more different personalities, each opposed to the others or ignorant of them. If one of them appears to be diabolical, Church authorities' only means of determining whether it's a case of possession are the same ones used to distinguish hysteria from possession.

The Church considers paranormal phenomena an indication of possession, while on the other hand, many physicians and psychiatrists reject them as misperceptions or hallucinations. Even those less skeptical, however, may not consider paranormal phenomena as the work of demons. But the Church's test is based on whether such phenomena occur in the context of a hateful aversion to religion.

THE BOOBY-TRAPPED TOMB

China's first emperor, Qin Shi-Huang-di, was entombed in a massive, intricate burial complex built especially for him. As described by historian Qian Sima in the second century B.C., the complex was surrounded by a river of mercury that was circulated manually.

Even though Qian Sima was the most famous of all Chinese historians and a highly regarded scholar, his descriptions of rivers of mercury and other details of the emperor's tomb were considered myths. Recent excavations in China, however, have tended to bear out much of what Qian had said. As reported in the *Guangming Daily,* the official Chinese newspaper, an analysis of the soil around the burial complex revealed unusually high levels of mercury.

In fact, Qian Sima's description of the tomb has become so believable that archaeologists excavating the tomb are now being very cautious. Qian, after all, had also warned that the burial ground was booby-trapped with "mechanically triggered crossbows set to shoot any intruder."

A DREAM OF ASSASSINATION

On May 3, 1812, British aristocrat John Williams dreamed he was in the cloak room of the British Parliament's House of Commons when he observed a crazed man in a green coat shoot and kill another man. When he asked the identification of the slain man, he was told it was Prime Minister Spencer Perceval. Awakening, the shaken Williams recounted the dream to his wife and then fell back to sleep. The nightmare recurred twice more before dawn, awakening him each time.

Not a particularly political man, Williams wondered about the meaning of the persistent dream, even debating whether he should warn the prime minister. Little did he know that Perceval had dreamed a similar scenario. In his recurring nightmare, the prime minister told his family in the morning, he was walking through the House of Commons lobby when he was accosted by a lunatic wearing a dark green jacket with shiny brass buttons. The man aimed and fired his pistol. Then, Perceval reported, everything went black.

Although his family tried to convince him to remain home, Perceval arrived at the House of Commons and, as he entered the lobby, was shot by a madman wearing a green coat with brass buttons.

REVENGE FROM BEYOND THE GRAVE

In 1681 a County Durham, England, miller named Jason Graeme was visited not once but three times by a female ghost bent on revenge. The apparition, who told Graeme her name was Anne Walker, presented a hideous appearance: Covered in blood, she had five gaping wounds in her head. She had become pregnant and then murdered, she said, by Mark Sharp, who had been hired by a relative who had caused Walker's pregnancy. The ghost now wanted Graeme to go to the authorities and tell them her story.

Refusing to believe that Anne was anything more than a disturbing figment of his imagination, Graeme did not comply with the request. And Anne Walker appeared twice more to plead her case before the miller went to the local magistrate, telling him the location where Sharp had buried the murder victim. When the pit was searched, a body was found, bearing the wounds as described by Graeme. As a result of the grisly discovery, the relative and Mark Sharp were arrested, tried, and hanged. Anne Walker had exacted her revenge.

THE MYSTERIOUS GREEK PLAGUE

Do diseases die out and become extinct? Or do they merely lie dormant, awaiting the conditions that will trigger their resurrection? A mysterious plague, for example, ravaged Athens between 430 and 427 B.C., leaving death and suffering in its wake, and so weakening the army that Athens was defeated in the war with Sparta. According to the Greek historian Thucydides, the symptoms included cough, vomiting, diarrhea, and thirst, as well as blisters, gangrene, and amnesia. Originating in Ethiopia, the disease, he wrote, spread through Egypt, Libya, Persia, and then struck Piraeus and Athens. For centuries, scholars have attempted to determine what the disease was.

Retired epidemiologist Alexander Langmuir, who formerly headed the epidemiology department of Atlanta's Center for Disease Control, reports that many of the symptoms cited by Thucydides resemble those of pandemic influenza, similar to the 1918 outbreak. But other symptoms, like convulsive retching and gangrene of the hands and toes, appear compatible with a staphylcoccus infection very much like today's toxic shock syndrome, considered a new disease. It raises the idea that the plague of Athens is not an extinct disease and could, in fact, erupt again in the future.

STAR MAPS OF THE SUMERIANS

The Babylonians have long been acknowledged for their vast celestial knowledge, developed thousands of years before the European astronomical revolution led by Copernicus. But newly translated Babylonian texts indicate that the civilization's wealth of information was actually inherited from the Sumerians who preceded them. The Babylonians, it seems, knew only how to use the Sumerian charts and actually understood very little if anything about the basis for the calculations.

The basis for our modern calendar, then, was developed some five thousand years ago by the Sumerians who recognized that the planets were spherical and revolved around the sun. And they understood that the earth wobbles on its axis, affecting the direction of the North Pole. And they calculated that it takes nearly twenty-six thousand years for the North Pole to return to the same position. Even more surprisingly, they precisely measured the distances between stars, valuable information for space travel. But why were the Sumerians, with no conceivable mode of interstellar transportation so interested in establishing the *distance* from one star to another?

FRIENDLY GHOSTS

According to Carol Mitchell at Colorado State University, most ghosts today are friendlier than in days gone by. In a survey of four hundred people who had encountered ghosts, Mitchell found that the otherworldly entities have become less outlandish and wild and more prosaic. Survey respondents described ghosts as blue or white lights, fireballs, or vague human figures that appeared briefly in a variety of settings, including cars, homes, and backyards, but particularly bedrooms. They would talk with family members, give advice, and even ask to hold children. The survey results refute the idea that ghostly encounters have decreased in recent years.

THE SCENT OF VIOLETS

After his disastrous performance in the Franco-Prussian War in 1870, Emperor Napoleon III and his family fled France for Great Britain, where they were given refuge by Queen Victoria. The emperor's son, Louis, became so attached to his adopted country that he volunteered for military service in South Africa. And in 1879, he gave up his life for England in the battle of Isandlahuana against the

Zulus. He was buried in the jungle not far from the site of his death, although no one was quite sure where.

Believing that her son should be interred in England in the family tomb, Empress Eugénie accompanied an 1880 expedition to find Louis's body. Day after day, the search party scoured the African jungle, unable to locate the burial site. Then, with her health affected by the tropical climate and her spirits sagging, the empress suddenly detected the scent of violets, her son's favorite flower. She followed the scent until it faded, at which point she stood directly over Louis's grave, overgrown and hidden in the jungle underbrush.

LEECH PRESCRIPTIONS

Before the dawn of twentieth-century medicine, physicians often used leeches to treat illness. Only now are modern doctors realizing that the bloodsuckers may be medically valuable. In fact, zoologist Roy Sawyer says the secretions from leeches will be to heart-related diseases what penicillin was to infectious diseases. They are already being used by plastic surgeons to restore healthy circulation in patients with skin grafts and reattached limbs. Two powerful enzymes in leech saliva can actually break down blood clots, and another could possibly cure glaucoma by attacking and destroying the buildup of the jelly behind the eye which causes the disease. Leeches are also helping researchers to learn more about Parkinson's disease. Nineteenth-century physicians and other medical practitioners may have actually guessed the beneficial possibilities of leeches even if they didn't understand fully how they affected the human body.

THE BISHOP AND THE ASSASSINATION OF THE ARCHDUKE

Bishop Joseph Lanyi awoke from a frighting dream involving a letter from his former student, the Archduke Francis Ferdinand of Austria. In the top margin of the stationery there was a small drawing of the archduke's car. A general sat opposite the ruler and his wife, and an officer was positioned next to the chauffeur. A crowd thronged the streets as two young men bearing guns approached the vehicle. Beneath the disturbingly detailed illustration, the text of the letter offered an eerier portent: "Dear Dr. Lanyi," it began, "I wish to inform you that my wife and I were the victims of a political assassination." It was signed "your Archduke Franz" and dated June 28, at 3:15 A.M.

According to the clock when the bishop awoke it was 3:15 in the morning and the date happened to be June 28, 1914. Writing down the details of the dreams, Lanyi later recounted the dream to his mother and others.

Around 3:30 that afternoon, Bishop Lanyi received a telegram with the news of Archduke Francis Ferdinand's assassination in Sarajevo, Yugoslavia, an event that triggered the outbreak of World War I. There had been only one murderer and the officer was standing on the car's running board, not next to the chauffeur, but otherwise, the details of the bishop's dream had been accurate.

CHINESE BIGFOOT

  Surrounded by the Chinese provinces of Hubei, Shaanxi, and Sichuan, the mountainous region of Shennongjia is apparently the home of a large, manlike beast, the Chinese counterpart to the American Sasquatch, or Bigfoot. In May 1976, six Communist party officials traveling by jeep through the southern part of Hubei came across the strange creature in the road ahead of them. It had fine, light brown body hair, with a dark red streak down the back, a humanlike face with a wide forehead and narrow chin, and a broad, gaping mouth. Motionless, it crouched in front of the vehicle and stared directly at the passengers. After they got out and surrounded it, throwing an occasional rock to prod it along, the creature finally rose on its long, muscular legs and lumbered silently off into the woods.

  Another sighting occurred a month later. Gong Yulan and her four-year-old son were gathering fodder for pigs when they saw a large animal with reddish colored hair rubbing its back against a tree less than twenty feet away. Yulan grabbed her child and ran, but, to her horror, the beast followed, screaming something that sounded like "Ya, ya."

  Numerous other reports of mysterious manlike creatures in the Shennongjian region, beginning in 1976, prompted the Chinese Academy of Sciences to organize an investigation. Searching and gathering evidence for eight months, 110 biologists, zoologists, photographers, and soldiers were never able to catch a specimen of the creature, but they did observe it. According to the leader of the research team, Ghou Guoting, the beast was neither human nor bear, but something in between, perhaps an as-yet-unidentified primate species. Archless footprints, measuring twelve to sixteen inches long, indicate that it has three distinct toes, one of which appears to be three digits grown together. And it is evidently not carnivorous, preferring to dine on nuts, leaves, roots, and insects.

DREAMY ENCOUNTERS WITH POSTMORTAL SOULS

Two Swiss researchers who have conducted a study of more than twenty-five hundred dreams believe that some nocturnal imaginings may actually be glimpses into the afterlife. Psychologists Maria-Louise von Franz and Emmanuel Xipolitas Kennedy have found that while not all dreams about life after death are significant, many have a special, supernatural quality that sets them apart. According to Kennedy, they appear to be encounters with postmortal souls much like those that typically occur among the terminally ill. The dreamers sometimes describe themselves as rejuvenated in their dreams, or they may meet up with close friends or relatives who have already passed away. Kennedy believes that even if not actually proof of life after death, these dreams have considerable value in confirming for the unconscious mind that impending death is not an end, which then eases the patient's passage from life into death. They point to the notion that whatever is unresolved during life must somehow, Kennedy asserts, be continued after death. The purpose is to somehow unite the individual with the archetypal being we think of as God.

DEATH BY OVERDOSE OF WATER

Tina Christopherson, a twenty-nine-year-old Florida woman with an I.Q. of 189, was obsessed with the idea that she had stomach cancer, the same disease that had killed her mother. To cleanse her body, she often went on water fasts, eating no food but drinking as much as four gallons of water a day. She eventually drank so much water that her kidneys were overwhelmed and the fluid began draining into her lungs. She died of internal drowning, or "water intoxication."

THE SPECTRAL SOLDIERS OF LOE BAR

In 1974, Stephen Jenkins returned to Loe Bar on the Cornish coast near where King Arthur is said to have died. Jenkins arrived with a map in his hand and his wife by his side. His first visit to the area had been in August 1936, as a teenager. At that time, he had been gazing around the landscape when he saw a battalion of medieval warriors, mounted on horseback and wearing cloaks of red, black, and white. One soldier stood in the center of the group, his hand on his sword, and stared directly at Jenkins. But when Jenkins moved forward to get a better look, the entire army vanished.

Now, the vision reappeared exactly as it had nearly four decades earlier, but this time, Jenkins's wife was also a witness. And with the map, he was able to pinpoint the exact rendezvous site of the spectral army. Plotting a grid between ancient burial grounds in the area, Jenkins concluded that the soldiers became visible only at the specific spot because of the psychic energy emanating from the surrounding burial grounds.

The Disappearing and Reappearing Spanish Mission

No one is exactly sure where the Mission of the Four Evangelists lies, but it's believed to be within a forty-mile radius of Yuma, Arizona, perhaps in the southwestern state itself. Many believe, however, that the Spanish mission probably rests alongside Laguna Prieta, a lake south of the border in Mexico, although no one can find the lake either. Hiding under the desert sands for years, the Spanish mission magically reappears only to disappear again. It may be covered by a natural phenomenon called "walking dunes," mounds of sand that form around objects and constantly change shape, occasionally reaching heights of three hundred feet or more.

THE TRAVELING JAPANESE

In more than fifty years of examining pre-Colombian art, Alejandro von Wuthenau has found dozens of statues with Asian features, some dating from 2000 B.C. One, for example, is a terra-cotta reproduction of an Asian wrestler dating between 1000 and 800 B.C. and found in the Mexican mountains of Guerrero. The artifacts, von Wuthenau insists, indicate that the Japanese visited the Americas long before Europeans did. The only question was, How did they get there?

In 1986, von Wuthenau discovered what he believes may be a replica of a seafaring vessel used by early Asian explorers. The foot-long terra-cotta boat contains ten figurines of oarsmen, all with distinctly Japanese faces.

THE MISSING MARINER

When *The Times* of London sponsored a round-the-world boat race, scheduled to begin on October 31, 1968, Donald Crowhurst thought the publicity not to mention the prize money would be ideal to give his failing business a shot in the arm. So the marine electronics entrepreneur entered the race with his newly built *Teignmouth*

Electron. Two weeks into the journey, however, he decided to loiter in the South Atlantic and fake his logbooks. Then, when it was apparent that only the *Teignmouth Electron* and one other ship remained in the race, Crowhurst decided that his only alternative was to let the other ship win. But on May 21, 1969, his sole rival went down near the Azores.

Distraught about the notoriety surrounding his victory revealing his fraud, Crowhurst seemed to lose his mind, as evidenced by the increasingly incoherent and rambling logbook entries and radio messages, which ceased on June 30. When the *Teignmouth Electron* was found adrift in the mid-Atlantic on July 11, Crowhurst was not on board. One theory suggests that he jumped overboard rather than face up to his "sin of concealment," as he called it in his logbook.

A TEST OF TELEPATHY

Before his flight to the Arctic by way of Alaska in October 1937, Sir Hubert Wilkins and Harold Sherman agreed to try communicating telepathically, setting up a strict experiment. For three thirty-minute periods, from 11:30 to midnight, Eastern Standard Time, on Monday, Tuesday, and Thursday evenings, Sherman would sit quietly and await Wilkins's messages. For his part, Wilkins would attempt to project information about what was happening to him during those particular periods. There would be two controls to ensure the test's legitimacy:

Each night Sherman would write down the impressions he received and mail them to Gardner Murphy, the head of Columbia University's department of parapsychology. And

Reginald Iverson, chief operator of *The New York Times* shortwave station, would report to Wilkins on the experiments' progress. A. E. Strath-Gordon and Henry Hardwicke observed Sherman on Wilkins's behalf.

The results: An amazing number of impressions recorded by Sherman of events during Wilkins's expedition as well as the flyer's personal thoughts and reactions were approximately correct and impossible to have been guesswork.

On March 14, for example, Sherman wrote: "Believe you discovered crack of framework in tail of fuselage which needed repair. Seem to see you manipulating hand pump of some sort in flight. One engine is emitting spouts of black smoke—uneven, choked sound—as though carburetor trouble."

According to his own daily records, Wilkins had, in fact, discovered the crack in the framework. His trouble with the engine, caused by changing from one gas tank to another, had occupied his mind all day.

Wilkins himself was surprised by some details in Sherman's reports, including the mental image Sherman received about Wilkins in evening attire at a ball in Saskatchewan. Of course there were times when Sherman received no telepathic messages and his impressions were wrong. But that he received anything was remarkable.

NATIVE AMERICAN FREEMASONS

In the mid-seventies, photographer and former newspaper publisher John Loughran was photographing Anasazi archaeological sites in the American Southwest when he noticed remarkable similarities between the Indians' men's temples and his own Masonic lodge. Well versed in the traditions and symbolism of Freemasonry, he realized that the Anasazi temple furniture was placed the same way, and the area in which the main rituals took place seemed 80 percent identical to contemporary American Masonic lodges. The only difference was that the Indian temple was round. After further research, however, Loughran discovered that the Masonic temples in northern Africa were initially round, too.

Loughran speculates that if Native Americans practiced Freemasonry, then they had to have possessed a written language, despite beliefs to the contrary, because Masonic doctrine is built on learning.

By using his knowledge of Freemasonry to decipher symbols left by the Anasazi, Loughran was able to follow clues to a hidden, ancient Indian library containing rock and clay tablets, ranging in size up to two feet by one foot and dated between A.D. 1000 and 1200. The most surprising find, however, is that they appear to have been written in a script resembling Arabic.

THE STRANGE LIGHTS OF THE MOON

Since the eighteenth century, astronomers have observed mysterious lights emanating from the surface of the moon, the earliest record dating to 1787. On the nights of April 19 and 20 of that year, British astronomer Sir William Herschel had directed his telescope on the moon and was surprised to detect three brightly shining lights, which he concluded came from lunar volcanoes. And in 1790, Herschel observed more than 150 of the same kind of lights that he described as "red, luminous points . . . small and round."

Even though Herschel was a respected scientist, his volcano theory was, for the most part, discounted. According to a report published in *The American Journal of Science and Arts* in 1822, lunar volcanoes were unlikely because any molten rock at the moon's core would cool rapidly due to the moon's size. Instead, it was postulated that the lights observed by Herschel and others near the crater Aristarchus were just reflections of light from earth.

By 1965, astronomer Zdenek Kopal had compiled sixteen separate cases of lights at the Aristarchus crater and other regions, but the source was still in dispute. Kopal was able to obtain pictures of the moon that showed a distinct brightening in dark areas of the surface. These he attributed to particles emitted by solar flares that had occurred shortly before. But Kopal could not apply the same explanation to the spots of light discerned in sunlit areas of the moon, leading him to the idea that "the effects of solar activity may depend on processes that are not yet understood."

A few years later, in the magazine *Nature*, A. A. Mills proposed another theory for the lunar lights: "Fluidized beds" of fine dust were being churned up by gases beneath the moon's surface. These beds would, in turn, give off a hazy "glow discharge" of static electricity that, from the earth, appeared to be points of light.

None of these hypotheses has yet been proven or disproven. Another observation of the lights defies all of them, however. In 1788, German astronomer Johann Hieronymus Schroter saw what he described as "a light point, as brilliant as a fifth-magnitude star" to the east of the lunar Alps. After fifteen minutes, the light simply disappeared. Schroter continued to observe the moon until the same area reappeared, this time in full sunlight. He was astonished to see a round black and gray shadow exactly where the light had been on the moon's previous revolution.

ANCIENT BUTTER BALL

From as early as the Middle Ages and until at least the nineteenth century, homemakers would store dairy products in Ireland's peat bogs. But no one has ever found anything quite like the ball of butter unearthed recently. Rancid but edible, the huge ball of butter weighed nearly a hundred pounds and lay buried at a depth of five feet, indicating that it's approximately 1,000 years old. Stored in what is believed to be the stomach of a cow, the butter was well preserved by the moist conditions of the bog. Like the discovery of the world's oldest preserved human brain matter in a watery burial ground in Florida, the find is another example of the incredible preservation potential of saturated soils.

Cold, moist mud and clay, well underground, has also preserved corpses from medieval and even ancient times. Unlike mummies, these frozen-mud corpses conserve the exact features of people as they appeared during their lifetime centuries ago. A few of these have been found under Polish marshes, and one in Denmark, apparently a criminal, was found with the hangman's noose still around his neck, his face contorted as at the moment of his death, about 1000 years ago.

PETS THAT SENSE EARTHQUAKES

The Chinese have long noted that animals can somehow sense an imminent earthquake. They sense the drastic changes in the earth's magnetic field, the precursors to earthquakes, and become nervous and frightened, often going into hiding.

Jim Berkland became convinced of the Chinese earthquake-warning wisdom, in part based on observations of animal behavior, when his own cat ran away right before a large earthquake. It returned a few months later—just before another quake. (In Japan, prior to earthquakes, goldfish have tried to jump out of their bowls and, in China, pet birds attempt to get out of their cages.)

Chief geologist for California's Santa Clara County, Berkland now goes through the lost-and-found classified sections of three California major newspapers, counting the number of missing cats and dogs. When the number of lost pets increases, it means the state may be hit by a quake.

He combines the number of animals advertised as missing, data on geyser and tidal activity, and the position of the sun and moon, periods when conditions are most favorable for earthquakes to occur. And he compares it all to make his earthquake predictions, boasting an 82 percent success rate.

MONTREAL'S DAY WITHOUT SUNSHINE

The morning of November 10, 1819, dawned dark and ominous in the city of Montreal, Quebec, Canada. When residents saw the heavy clouds that quickly changed from a murky green to pitch black, they expected a repeat of the thick, soapy rain that had left behind a sooty residue two days before. They were unprepared, however, for the mysterious and terrifying bout of violent weather that ensued, the likes of which had never been seen before or since.

By noon of that Tuesday, the lights throughout the city were lit and shining as if it were night. The sun, when it could be seen through the thick clouds, ranged from a dark brown color to a sickly yellow, to orange, and finally to blood red. At about two in the afternoon, a wave of clouds rushed over the city, followed by a glaring flash of lightning that illuminated the sky like the sun. Then thunder rattled windows and shook the buildings to their foundations.

Another rush of clouds came, and then a light rain, similar to the shower that fell two days earlier, began to fall. Terrified residents watched as the next blaze of lightning struck the spire of the French parish church. Electricity danced around the iron cross atop the ball at the steeple's summit. The cross plummeted to the ground and shattered.

When residents awoke the next morning, however, the sky was clear and blue. The only trace of the storm was the broken cross lying on the ground.

THE MAN IN THE BLACK
VELVET MASK

In 1848, Alexandre Dumas wrote the classic novel *The Man in the Iron Mask,* based on a true but mysterious incident that took place during the reign of Louis XIV of France in the seventeenth century. In Dumas's tale, a man was secretly held prisoner for thirty-four years in a variety of prison suites, and wore an iron mask to conceal his identity. The prisoner, according to Dumas, was the king's twin brother, whose face would have been recognizable to anyone who saw it. In reality, however, the historical identity of the prisoner has never been determined.

What is known? In July 1669, a man was captured near Dunkirk. Apparently too dangerous to set free and, for some reason, too valuable to kill, he was imprisoned in the Bastille, where he lived in solitary confinement until he died in 1703, probably of natural causes. And unlike the character in Dumas's story, the historic prisoner wore a black velvet mask, not an iron one.

Some people believe the man in the black velvet mask was the king's older brother, imprisoned to avoid disputes over who was the rightful heir to the throne. Still others surmise that he was Louis himself, his throne usurped by an impostor, an illegitimate half-brother. But perhaps the most feasible explanation is that he was Louis's real father.

Louis's parents had been estranged for many years when the future king was born in 1683. And Louis XIII, moreover, was old, ailing, and probably impotent. With the need for an heir to succeed the king, royal advisers might have provided the queen with a surrogate husband. If, then, the prisoner was Louis's biological father, and if the son had him executed, it would have been akin to patricide. And Louis probably did not have anything against him. But imprisoned, ordered by royal decree to speak to no one (and others ordered not to listen) under pain of death, the man could not reveal Louis XIV's true heritage.

THE CURSE OF THE CHARLES HASKELL

Fishermen are a superstitious lot, and those who ply their trade in the particularly treacherous waters of Grand Banks off the coast of Newfoundland may be a bit warier than most. So when a workman inspecting the schooner *Charles Haskell* slipped off a companionway and broke his neck in 1869, many decided the boat was cursed. But despite the reputation, Captain Curtis of Gloucester, Massachusetts, assumed command, and eventually managed to assemble a crew willing to sail the *Haskell*.

In 1870, the *Charles Haskell* was among the hundred or so vessels in the waters of the Grand Banks when a hurricane struck. While the sea churned and the fishing ships pitched, the *Haskell* rammed the *Andrew Johnson*, destroying it and killing everyone on board. Although heavily damaged, the *Haskell* managed to limp back to port.

Repairs made, the *Haskell* ventured back out into the Grand Banks again the following spring. Six days after setting sail, two men on midnight watch duty experienced a horrifying vision: twenty-six phantoms in rain slickers boarded the vessel. Their eyes hollow sockets, they proceeded to take up their positions as if to commence fishing. Some time later, their mission evidently completed, the ghostly fishermen returned, single file, to the murky waters.

The watchmen reported what they had seen to the captain who, sufficiently alarmed by the guards' terrified faces, turned the boat around. But on their way home, the fishing apparitions appeared once again. This time, as the *Haskell* approached shore, the twenty-six marine ghosts walked over the water toward the port of Salem.

That was all it took to convince the fishermen, including Captain Curtis, and the *Charles Haskell* never sailed again.

WALDO'S MOUNTAIN

In the early sixties, an eccentric land developer named Waldo Sexton decided his hometown of Vero Beach, Florida, was far too flat. What it needed was a mountain. So he built one. On the sides of the fifty-foot-high hill, Sexton carved steps that led to two solitary lawn chairs perched on the summit. Sexton later donated his mountain to the city for the enjoyment—and the amusement—of everyone.

When the mountain was leveled in 1972, just five years after Sexton's death, a restaurant was built in its place. But ever since it opened, the restaurant has been plagued by strange happenings. Glasses broke and objects fell off the walls for no apparent reason. One night, after the proprietor Loli Heuser had closed the restaurant and saw a vision of a bronze statue of Waldo Sexton himself, she thought she understood what was affecting the restaurant. Waldo, disturbed by the razing and replacement of his mountain, had been exacting his annoying revenge.

Heuser's solution to the problem? Hoping to appease the deceased land developer, she plans to erect a statue of Waldo Sexton and a miniature replica of his mountain on the restaurant's grounds.

INSTILLING THE FEAR OF DEATH

A most bizarre method of execution was perfected by Australian aborigines. The ritual, called bone-pointing, was brought to national attention in 1953 when Kinjika, a tribal member of the Mailli in Arnhem Land, was hospitalized in Darwin. Although he had no symptoms of poisoning, disease, or assault, the aborigine died after four days of intense suffering.

Kinjika had fled his homeland after being condemned to death by the Mailli tribal council for breaking the taboo of incest. In an elaborate ritual, the executioner began preparing the *kundela,* or killing bone, derived from a human, kangaroo, or emu. Sometimes even made out of wood, the kundela is six to nine inches long and usually includes a tail of human hair. When fashioned, it's then charged with powerful psychic energy.

Since Kinjika had left the confines of the village, the ritual executioners, or *kurdaitcha,* were enlisted to find and kill the convicted man. Traditional kurdaitcha, covered in human blood and kangaroo hair, travel in pairs or threesomes, wearing masks made of emu feathers and slippers that allow them to tread silently. When they find their victim, they pose as if ready to shoot but, instead, merely point the kundela, utter a chant, and then depart.

Whether, in fact, the result of the bone's psychic energy or his mental state, the victim is left a pitiful sight, imagining the lethal weapon's venom pouring into him. His eyes glaze over, his face becomes horribly distorted, his muscles twitch uncontrollably. He may froth at the mouth while attempting to scream, the sounds caught in his throat. He becomes increasingly sick and lethargic, refusing to eat, and inevitably dies within days.

Only one thing can alter the effects of bone-pointing and that is a countercharm administered by the tribe's medicine man.

WHEN GALAXIES COLLIDE

Of all the scenarios for an apocalyptical end to the world, the grandest is probably a catastrophic collision between our Milky Way and another galaxy. Astronomer Marshal McCall, in fact, has estimated the likelihood of such an event actually occurring and, he's determined, it will, although not in our lifetimes.

The Milky Way is linked by gravity to a neighboring galaxy known to astronomers as simply M31. With their common center of gravity, their present course will bring them together, McCall speculates, in about four million years. All the planets in our solar system, however, will remain clinging to the sun because their gravitational bonds are stronger than the intergalactic forces.

At worst, perhaps, our solar system could be ripped out of the Milky Way and sent on an independent course through space.

THE CURSE OF DUNNELLEN HALL

After her husband died of a heart attack while being driven home by their chauffeur, Lynda Dick put the twenty-eight-room Dunnellen Hall up for sale. She compared the Greenwich, Connecticut, mansion to the Hope Diamond, and told the real estate agent that it brought bad luck to everyone who owned it. Indeed, since it passed out of the hands of the original family owners, most of the occupants have suffered financial difficulties, with some being indicted.

Dunnellen Hall, a Jacobean mansion on twenty-six acres of land with a view of Long Island Sound, was built in 1918, commissioned by Daniel Grey Reid as a wedding present for his daughter Rhea and her husband, Henry Ropping. In 1950, their sons sold the estate to Loring Washburn, president of a steel-fabricating company.

In 1963, after Washburn suffered financial difficulties, Dunnellen was taken over by a finance company and remained vacant until bought by Gregg Sherwood Dodge Moran; a showgirl and former wife of an heir to the Dodge automobile fortune, she married Daniel Moran, a New York City police officer who later shot himself.

Financier Jack Dick paid $1 million for Dunnellen Hall in 1968. Soon after, in 1971, he was indicted and charged with stealing $840,000 through the false use of documents to obtain a loan. He died in 1974, before the case went to trial.

Despite Lynda Dick's conclusion about the estate's being cursed, the price for Dunnellen Hall increased to $3 million when India-born oil supertanker owner Ravi Tikkoo bought it in 1974. A slump in the oil market during the oil embargo of the mid-seventies forced Tikkoo to sell the property to its most recent owners, real estate and hotel tycoon Harry Helmsley and his wife, Leona. In 1988, the Helmsleys were indicted on federal charges of evading more than $4 million in income taxes. In 1989 Leona Helmsley was convicted of the charges of tax evasion and sentenced to a prison term.

SOUTH AMERICAN SUPER SNAKES

Some of the longest snakes ever reported made their homes in the Amazon River basin of Brazil. In the early twentieth century, for example, two reputable observers spotted monster serpents and took their tales back to civilization. But sometimes no matter how reliable the witness, people refuse to believe.

In 1907, for example, Col. Henry Fawcett was surveying the Amazon basin for the Royal Geographical Society. He and his Indian crew were making their way down the Rio Abunhã when the triangular head of an anaconda appeared below their boat's bow. Fawcett grabbed his rifle and fired a bullet into the reptile's spine. There was a sudden flurry of foam and a thumping against the boat's keel before the snake died, its body continuing to undulate with ghastly tremors. Fawcett estimated the snake's length to be sixty-two feet—seventeen feet in the water, with another forty-five still on shore.

An even larger water snake was sighted by Victor Heinz,

a Brazilian missionary, on May 22, 1922, at three o'clock in the afternoon. Heinz was traveling up the flood-swelled Amazon when he was startled by a huge shape thirty yards ahead. It was a giant water snake, wrapped into two coils and drifting placidly downstream. As thick as an oil drum, its visible length was roughly eighty feet.

The priest and his crew passed the snake, keeping silent and trying not to rock the boat too much with their collective trembling. When the vessel was clear of the monstrous reptile, one of the guides explained that the reason the snake was so calm was because it had just feasted on several enormous rodents known as capybaras.

KING SOLOMON'S MINES

According to the Bible, King Solomon was phenomenally rich, and clearly imported most of his precious metals and stones, as well as other exotica and luxuries, from far distant lands. Much of it is now thought to have been copper or brass, and mystery shrouds the location of the fabled mines.

The Bible's clues focus on two places, Ophir, where the gold came from, and Tarshish, connected with the navy that collected it. Unfortunately, there's no indication of the city's location. There are a number of possibilities, at least for Tarshish: First, there may have been more than Tarshish (which can be translated as "smeltery") where Solomon obtained his metals. Or Jewish historian Josephus, who translated the Old Testament in the first century A.D., actually meant Tarsus, an ancient Roman port. But since Solomon was linked with the sea-trading Phoenicians, who colonized what is now Spain, Tarshish might be Tartessos, a kingdom near Cadiz and described by the Greeks as being rich in silver.

Tartessos may have been the starting point for even greater sea adventures around Africa and, maybe, America. Voyages to the Western Hemisphere are a possibility, made more tantalizing by the discovery on the Mediterranean coast of Israel of a text that mentions the "gold of Ophir" and suggests that Ophir could be reached via Gibraltar. The Phoenicians, then, may have visited Brazil, which means "Iron" in Aramaic and Hebrew, a striking example of an ancient name being applied to a land and its chief product *before* the country was "officially" discovered by later explorers.

THE WALKING DEAD

In Haiti, the blending of African religions and European catholicism resulted in a curious spiritual amalgam known as voodoo. The *loas,* or gods, imbue the priests, in particular, with special powers that enable them to reanimate supposed corpses into the mindless automatons of zombies.

Some of the most striking zombie manifestations are the result of love or revenge, which play major roles in the practice of voodoo. In one recorded case, a voodoo priest, or *houngan,* attempted to possess a young woman who was engaged to marry another man. She rebuffed the houngan's advances, and the angry priest was heard muttering threats and curses as he departed the woman's company. Within a few days, the woman fell mysteriously ill and died. When the body was being prepared for burial, her head had to be tilted slightly so that she would completely fit inside the coffin. And someone also inadvertently burned her foot with a cigarette.

Not long after the funeral, it was rumored that the woman had been seen with the very same houngan she had previously rejected. There was no concrete evidence, however, and the possibility of her being alive wasn't pursued. Then, years later, the dead woman returned to her home, telling the family she'd been turned into a zombie by the voodoo priest, but was released when the houngan repented. She was positively identified by the scar from the cigarette burn on her foot and by her neck permanently bent from her placement in the coffin.

THE LEGEND OF COUNT SAINT-GERMAIN

He was an adviser to kings, a social celebrity, an alchemist, and a wise man of great repute. But everything about the man known as the Count (of) Saint-Germain is shrouded in mystery. It's not known, for example, where or when he was born, or when he died. There are some, in fact, who believe Count Saint-Germain is still alive.

A vibrant conversationalist, a talented violinist, a skilled painter, and incredibly knowledgeable in every conceivable subject, Count Saint-Germain first became a celebrity during the mid-eighteenth century through his close association with Louis XV of France. Some called the count a genius;

others believed him to be a charlatan of considerable proportions. He was especially mistrusted by members of the king's court who envied the count's position as royal confidant. Saint-Germain even involved himself in foreign policy decisions, to the chagrin of the rest of the government. Under the threat of arrest, Count Saint-Germain fled to England.

It was commonly believed that Saint-Germain was also a member of a secret society, perhaps the Freemasons or Rosicrucians and was familiar with the ancient rites. Some fifteen years before the French revolution, he warned the king of the coming bloodbath. And in addition to telling the future, the count was also a historian who recounted events as if he had been there.

Saint-Germain's death, moreover, is as mysterious as his life had been. According to court records, the count died on February 27, 1784. At the time, he was practicing alchemy with Prince Charles of Hessen-Kassel in Germany, and later whenever he was asked about his friend's death, the prince would always change the subject, as if trying to cover up something. In fact, Saint-Germain was registered at a convention of Freemasons in 1785, and was cited by reputable sources in Vienna and the Far East as late as the 1800s.

CATTLE MUTILATIONS

Satanic cultists or UFOs? It's a question cattle ranchers in the American Midwest have often pondered following numerous incidents of bizarre mutilations among their herds. Whatever the answer, something destroyed their cattle in a grisly and puzzling manner.

In late summer of 1975, a Colorado rancher found a blue plastic valise containing a cow's ear and tongue as well as a scalpel. This was viewed by investigators as the first concrete clue linking the killings to some kind of cult. Then in August of that year, a motorist in Blaine County, Idaho, reported seeing a group of hooded figures near a ranch where two cows were found mutilated the following day. Subsequent searches failed to turn up any further signs of cultists. Even so, investigators were convinced that the culprits were human, even if their activities were inhumane.

Other incidents, however, were not so practically explained. In Washington County, Colorado, for example, mutilated cattle seemed to have been dropped from the sky, leading ranchers to the conclusion that aircraft were involved. And in Copperas Cove, Texas, a farmer saw an orange light hovering over his farm on the night his calves were butchered. The following day, inspection of the area revealed that the grass was flattened in concentric circles, as if pressed down by a blast of air from above.

One of the most puzzling cattle mutilations took place in Whiteface, Texas, in March, 1975. Not only was the heifer found in the center of a scorched circle of wheat, but the mutilation was particularly horrible and inexplicable. The animal's tongue and external organs had been removed; its neck was grotesquely twisted; and its navel appeared to have been bored out. Yet amazingly, there were no signs of blood anywhere on the ground around the animal.

THE HERMIT CZAR

Almost immediately after it was announced that Russian czar Alexander I had died at the age of forty-seven, people began wondering if he was, indeed, dead. Rumors spread that he had actually abdicated in order to live the life of a hermit. Residents of Tomsk, in fact, claimed that a hermit named Fedor Kuzmich had suddenly appeared in their eastern Russia town and was really the former czar. When Kuzmich died in 1864, moreover, his last words were "God knows my real name."

Having become czar following the death of his father, Alexander II attempted to put an end to the stories about his father. In 1865, he ordered the casket opened, but found it empty. A subsequent examination in 1926 confirmed that the body was not inside the casket.

THE MAN WHO WITNESSED HIS OWN FUNERAL

An anonymous English victim of typhoid fever was exhumed four days after his burial in 1831 and taken to a group of medical students for dissection. When the professor began cutting into the chest, however, the corpse cried out and grabbed the professor's arm. The events leading up to his assumed death make his story even more bizarre.

Although his physical strength declined as a result of the typhoid fever, the Englishman explained, he had never lost his mental awareness. Unable to speak or otherwise communicate, he heard the doctor pronounce him dead and felt his face being covered. He lay alert as family and friends mourned for three days. Following what he called brutal treatment by the undertaker, he "heard the crashing of the wood as they drove in the nails fastening the lid. Crammed into that narrow box, I experienced a sensation as if my head and limbs were being torn asunder." Then he heard a friend reading the graveside sermon.

He remained alert during the next four days. But when the professor's knife began to cut him, though, "I succeeded in crying out, the bonds of death were separated, and I returned to life."

DID ACID RAIN KILL THE DINOSAURS?

Today's acid rain is about as strong as vinegar. It may not burn holes in your clothes, but it can kill trees and fish by slowly changing the mineral concentrations in soil and water. Ronald Prinn and Bruce Fegley, Jr., of the Massachusetts Institute of Technology, however, speculate that prehistoric acid rain was much stronger, about the same as strong laboratory acid, and would have attacked plants and animals, devastating life in the oceans as well as on land. So if dust clouds from an asteroid didn't wipe out the dinosaurs sixty-five million years ago, perhaps Prinn and Fegley's acid rain did.

Scientists almost always find high levels of the rare metal iridium in stratified layers of sediment laid down about sixty-five million years ago. Based on known concentrations of iridium in asteroids and comets, scientists speculate that a small asteroid or a large comet struck the earth at that time, creating a cloud of debris that dusted the planet with iridium.

Dr. Luis Alvarez, of the Lawrence Berkeley Laboratory (California) has signalized an iridium layer in rock layers of the Mesozoic era (sixty-five million years ago). This layer has been found in various parts of the world and has been called the layer of the "Great Dying," a cemetery marker for the enormous dinosaurs who had held dominion over the earth for millions of years.

The comet, with much lower concentrations of iridium, would have had to be about twenty times larger than the asteroid. The impact, then, would have heated up the earth's atmosphere, turning nitrogen and oxygen into nitrous oxide. This would have combined with rain to produce nitric acid, or very acid rain.

WOLF CHILDREN OF INDIA

The Reverend J. A. L. Singh had heard many tales about the man-beasts said to live among the wolves. And the wolves, the people said, made their den in a defunct termite mound. After Singh himself saw one of the creatures, he decided to investigate further, returning to the site with a hired crew to dig into the mound. It was not long before several wolves escaped their threatened den. One of them attacked the crew who shot and killed it. With the wolves gone, however, the crew continued digging until they made a shocking discovery: Deep within the mound, they found two human children, one about two years old, the other approximately eight. The two little girls were curled up with two wolf cubs as if they were all siblings.

Singh took the girls, who he named Kamala and Amala, back to the orphanage he administered in Midnapore, India. The feral children walked on their hands and feet, as if they were four-legged animals. They howled and would eat only meat. And civilized life was fatal for them. Amala, the younger child, died less than a year after they were rescued from the wolves. Nine years later, Kamala, having learned to walk upright and able to speak a few simple phrases, was also dead.

AND NO TIME OFF FOR GOOD BEHAVIOR

It was once common practice for Mediterranean countries to use convicts to man the oars of their warships. So in 1684, seventeen-year-old Jean Baptiste Mouron was convicted of incendiarism and sentenced to a hundred years and a day as a galley slave. Most of his time in the galleys, however, wasn't spent rowing, since galley ships had practically ceased by the time of Mouron's incarceration. The ships were moored as prison hulks. So Mouron was chained to a bench below the decks and left to rot along with the ship. Even so, he served his term in full, oddly enough, and finally tottered ashore a free man at the age of 117.

THE MYSTERY OF THE JOYITA

At dawn on October 3, 1955, the seventy-ton vessel *Joyita* left the port of Apia in Western Samoa, bound for the Tokelau Islands, 270 miles to the north. It was found thirty-seven days later 450 miles west of Samoa, its captain, crew, and passengers mysteriously missing. The boat's provisions, logbook, and instruments were gone, but on deck were a doctor's scalpel, stethoscope, and bloodstained bandages. A canvas awning had been draped over the front of the bridge.

One theory about the deserted boat proposed that the *Joyita* was rammed by Malay pirates or by a Japanese fishing vessel, its crew then looting the *Joyita* and murdering everyone on board. Another possibility was that those aboard had been kidnapped by extraterrestrials. Perhaps the most plausible idea was that the captain and a crewman had fought. The mate had fallen overboard and the injured captain had been treated by one of the passengers who happened to be a doctor. Threatened by a heavy storm and unable to navigate the ship, the crew and passengers climbed into the lifeboats, after rigging the awning above the captain, who refused to abandon the boat. Then the *Joyita* was discovered by fishermen who looted it and threw the dead or dying captain overboard.

The *Joyita*, however, was not licensed to carry passengers, and it's not known if there ever were any lifeboats. Although unseaworthy, the boat, moreover, held 640 cubic feet of cork in its hold during the voyage, making it unsinkable. It would, therefore, not have been necessary for anyone to abandon her.

THE PLANET OF BETHLEHEM

Astronomers have long sought a realistic explanation for the appearance of the Star of Bethlehem that heralded the birth of Jesus Christ and led the three Magi to his manger. Now, Roger Sinnott, an associate editor at *Sky and*

Telescope, explains that the appearance of the biblical star was really the result of Jupiter's and Venus's orbits converging in the year 2 B.C.

While the Jupiter and Venus convergence is well known, astronomers discounted it as the Star of Bethlehem. They argue that if it came to pass in 2 B.C., as Sinnott says, then it would have occurred after the death of King Herod, which presumably occurred in 4 B.C. According to biblical historians, however, King Herod was still alive at the time of Christ's birth.

But Sinnott believes that the problem lies in a miscalculation of the date for Herod's death. The ancient Jewish historian Flavius Josephus reported that Herod died around the time of the lunar eclipse. To most modern astronomers, that would date his death March 12, 4 B.C. Another eclipse, however, occurred on January 9, in the year 1 B.C. And if Herod died at the time of the second eclipse, he would still have been alive at the time of the Jupiter-Venus convergence, or the biblical Star of Bethlehem.

THE LEFT-HANDED ANTANALAS

At least 10 percent of the world's population is left-handed, sometimes considered an affliction in a world dominated by right-handed people. Because left-handedness is often considered sinister, many children have been pressured to become right-handed, but parents' and others' efforts have usually failed.

The Antanalas, therefore, are remarkable among the

world's races and cultures: the forest tribe of Madagascar is a left-handed society. In a complete reversal to the rest of the world, right-handedness is so rare that a child suspected of such a deviation from the norm would in former days be destroyed.

PREHISTORIC DENTAL FLOSS

The common image of Neanderthal man is still one of an unattractive half-beast. But he may have been hygienic enough to clean his teeth after every meal. Neanderthal teeth from a site near Krapina, Yugoslavia, were grooved with tiny but regular channels running from the front of the teeth to the back. Because the channels are so symmetrical, they couldn't have been formed by natural things like cavities and plaque which are lumpy and irregular.

THE DISAPPEARANCE OF FRIESLAND

For at least a hundred years, from the 1550s to the 1660s, the skilled craftsmen of Friesland traded with Greenland and Europe. But in the late seventeenth century, the large, well-populated island south of Greenland inexplicably disappeared from most maps. Some say the land mass sank, but if so, no one knows why. Others speculate that it was taken off the maps after being mistaken for a nearby island that did sink, which would mean that the island of Friesland should still exist, somewhere, if anyone can find it.

THE ABOMINABLE SNOWMAN
ON FILM

Photographer Anthony Wooldridge was on an assignment in the Himalayas for the British journal *Wildlife* when he spotted a large, furry animal among the snowy slopes. Of course, Wooldridge had heard all the legends about the yeti, or the Abominable Snowman, said to inhabit the mountainous region. It was a revelation to the photographer, however, to actually see a creature who could only be a mythological beast.

The creature was at least six feet tall, Wooldridge said, and "its head was large, and the whole body appeared to be covered with dark hair." Grateful for the once-in-a-lifetime opportunity, Wooldridge snapped several pictures of the yeti before it vanished into the Himalayan highlands.

Before *BBC Wildlife* editors would publish the photographs, of course, they submitted them to close scrutiny by two yeti experts. Both men agreed that the creature was unusual, although they differed in their opinions about what it actually was. In the opinion of Robert Martin, of University College in London, the figure could have been a "large primate as yet undocumented by zoologists." But anatomy expert and notorious skeptic John Napier shocked the editors by asserting his belief that the creature in the photo was definitely humanoid, neither bear nor human.

FISH THAT ATTACK SHARKS AND WIN

Sharks strike fear into most people, their great tearing muscular jaws being able to rip apart the heftiest of humans. But the little urchin-fish, or Sea Hedgehog, of South America frequently attacks and destroys sharks as long as twenty-five feet. With its flabby skin, speckled with spiny points, it can distend itself into a globular form, causing the spines to project like the quills of a porcupine. When swallowed by a shark, moreover, the urchin-fish eats and bores its way out, not only through the stomach wall, but completely through the side of the marine animal.

TRACK OF THE DEVIL

Residents of Devonshire in rural England awoke on the morning of February 8, 1855, to discover their snow-covered yards filled with mysterious hoofprints, shaped like tiny horseshoes and covering an area of a hundred miles.

Oddly, the tracks ran in a completely straight line, as if whatever made them had only one foot. Found throughout eighteen separate communities, the prints traced a path across fields and streams, up walls, and over rooftops. The countryfolk were certain that they were the tracks of Satan himself and, for some time thereafter, refused to venture out-of-doors after dark.

THE DAY THE SUN ROSE TWICE

By solving an ancient Chinese mystery, scientists have been able to determine how long days were nearly three thousand years ago. And time, it seems, does march on, because the days back then weren't exactly the same as they are today.

According to the "Bamboo Annals," the day dawned twice at a place called Zheng in the spring of the first year of the reign of King Y. In fact, the sun was eclipsed just before it rose above the horizon. People in Zheng saw the sky lighten before dawn, then turn dark as the moon passed in front of the sun. The end of the solar eclipse was the "second" dawn.

Grave robbers found the annals, written on sticks of bamboo and listing events beginning about 2000 B.C., in the tomb of King Hsiang, where they were buried in 299 B.C. Modern astronomers now study them for their records of ancient events. The annals also list earlier eclipses, but in the days before clocks, none were timed accurately. The daybreak eclipse at Zheng is an exception because astronomers can calculate the time of dawn.

An eclipse on April 21, 899 B.C., it turns out, matches the ancient Zheng account. But if the length of the day had remained unchanged at twenty-four hours, the eclipse would have been seen in the Middle East, not in China. It was seen in China, however, because the days in 899 B.C. were about 0.043 seconds shorter than today. Over a million days, that adds up to nearly six hours, enough to move the eclipse a quarter of the way around the earth, where the ancient Chinese saw it as a double.

THE MISSING FINANCIER AND THE PATIENT WIFE

On his way home one night in 1936, financier Fred Lloyd shared a taxi with a friend. Dropping his companion off in mid-Manhattan, Lloyd bade him farewell and continued uptown in the same cab. But Lloyd was never seen again.

Despite the fact that subsequent searches proved fruitless, Lloyd's wife spent the rest of her life steadfastly believing that her husband would return. When she died in 1945, Lloyd's three life insurance policies were found, still uncashed.

MONSTER RATS

In a bizarre twist of nature, giant rats, some weighing more than twenty-six pounds, were killing and eating cats in Iran. And according to the newspaper *Kayhan*, the rodents' extremely large hind legs enabled them to hop like kangaroos.

Bowling Green State University biology professor William Jackson believes the monster rats are similar to "cane cutters," large rats frequently found and even eaten in West Africa. But the African rodents are vegetarians, and Jackson is, therefore, baffled by the rats' need for meat. The rats' aggressive behavior, he says, is "very strange."

THE MYSTERIOUS MURDER IN A LOCKED ROOM

When Mrs. Locklan Smith heard screaming and obvious sounds of a struggle coming from New York City's Fifth Avenue Laundry, she called the police. When the officers arrived, however, they found the premises locked up tight—from the inside—except for an open transom. So they lifted a small boy through the window and he was able to crawl in and open the door.

Inside, the police found the laundry's proprietor, Isidore Fink, lying on the floor. He had been shot twice in the chest and once through the left hand, powder burns surrounding the bullet holes. The cash register and Fink's pockets, moreover, were full of money. But the motive for Fink's murder wasn't the only obvious mystery.

Fink always bolted the laundry's door when he worked at night. The only way his murderer could have gained access was if Fink let him in. But, with the door locked from the inside, the only exit would have been the transom which even a small child had difficulty squeezing through. And the powder burns indicated Fink was shot at close range, ruling out the theory that the gun had been fired from outside the window.

After two years of speculation, New York police commissioner Edward Mulrooney was forced to conclude that the Isidore Fink homocide was "an insoluble mystery."

THE FATAL SALUTE

In July of 1750, Robert Morris had a disturbing dream: he envisioned himself fatally wounded by cannon fire from the ship he was actually scheduled to visit the following day. When he awoke, the colonial dignitary was so petrified that he refused to board the vessel. Seeking to assuage his guest's fear, the ship's captain promised that there would be no gunfire from the ship until Morris was safely back on shore. Morris finally relented and the tour took place.

When the event was concluded, the captain, true to his word, ordered his men to hold off firing the cannon salute until he received word that Morris had arrived safely back on shore. While he was waiting, however, a fly landed on his nose and he raised his hand to brush it away. Taking the gesture as their cue, the crewmen fired the cannon. A fragment from the exploding cannonball struck Morris in the rowboat not far from his destination.

Despite the precautionary measures, his dreams had proved prophetic.

THE MISSING RING

In 1941, A. A. Vial of Greytown, Natal, South Africa, baked 150 cakes for the troops in war-torn Europe. After she was done, she realized her wedding ring was missing from her finger and concluded that it must have slipped into one of the cakes. To avoid destroying 150 cakes to find it, she sent them off to the army with a note in each one to please return her ring if found. The finder, it turned out, was her own son, who by extraordinary coincidence was handed one of the cakes and found his mother's ring in it.

A BIBLICAL ARTIFACT IN A MASSACHUSETTS ROCK?

In 1851, workmen were blasting solid rock in Dorchester, Massachusetts, when they made a curious discovery: a four-and-a-half-inch-high vase, split in half by the force of the explosion. What was unusual about the object, however, was that it was made of some unknown material artfully decorated with floral inlays of silver. The editor of *Scientific American*, writing at a time when Bible study was more popular, offered the possibility that the vase had been made by Tubal-cain, the biblical father of metallurgy.

HER FATHER'S EVIL SPIRIT

The blasphemous voices and strange abilities of an American woman identified only as Mary had begun manifesting themselves when she was a girl of fourteen. During the ensuing twenty-six years, doctors had diagnosed her as "normal in the fullest sense," although they couldn't explain her bizarre personality quirks. Consulting priests, moreover, were spat on and cursed by some entity controlling the woman's words and actions. Finally, at the age of forty, Mary was taken to a Franciscan monastery in Earling, Iowa, to see Theophilus Reisinger, a sixty-year-old monk well-versed in the ritual of exorcism.

The demon possessing Mary's body fought the monk's efforts, writhing, contorting, screeching inhumanly, and disgorging huge quantities of malodorous vomit and feces. It spoke in strange languages and spouted profanities and blasphemies at Reisinger and the others gathered in the room. At one point, the demon even predicted the car accident a few days later that killed Father Joseph Steiger, the convent's pastor assisting Reisinger. Yet Mary's lips never moved and, in fact, she remained unconscious throughout the ordeal.

The harrowing exorcism continued for months, during which time Reisinger was able to identify more than one malevolent spirit inhabiting Mary's body. The leader was named Beelzebub, but he was joined by Jacob, Mary's father, who instigated the possession, having cursed his daughter for refusing his incestuous advances. Jacob's mistress, Mina, was also among the demonic entities, damned she told Reisinger, for murdering four of her own children.

The exorcism was finally completed two days before Christmas, 1928, when Reisinger was able to expel the demons as they babbled so piercingly that the room vibrated with the sounds.

THE PSYCHOSOMATIC CURSE

Believers in the power of witch doctors and other practitioners of evil can be easily influenced by the power of suggestion. While curses in themselves may not be able to cause actual physical harm, the victims suffer very real psychosomatic effects from believing that evil can kill them. In the early part of the twentieth century, for example, a missionary was aided in his efforts to convert the Australian aborigines by a young convert named Rob. The aborigine convert would make frequent visits to a pocket of natives living on the outskirts of the community and led by a witch doctor named Nebo.

One day in 1919, a doctor from the International Health Division of the Rockefeller Foundation was summoned to the mission, where Rob lay ill. Despite obvious indications that Rob was seriously ill, however, there was no pain, fever, or other symptoms and no organic cause for the young aborigine's ailment. Based on Rob's claim that an angry Nebo had cursed him, the doctor and the missionary went to Nebo, threatening to cut off his food supply and drive him and his people from their homes if Rob died. Nebo consented to talk to Rob and told him that there had been a misunderstanding and that he had not cursed the man at all. Within moments, Rob rose from his bed, completely free of illness.

YOGI BODY HEAT

One of the most amazing things about Tibetan yogis is their ability to remain comfortable while living in high-altitude caves, where the temperatures are well below the tolerance level for most people. And the yogis do it while wearing the thinnest of garments or nothing at all. The key, of course, is *tumo*, a mystical heat or warmth. Attaining it is a highly guarded secret among the Tibetan priests, but it is a standard part of yoga training.

A neophyte monk who believes he has the ability to warm himself from within is put through a curious ritualistic test. During the night he is taken to a frozen river or lake where he is required to sit naked on the banks. Holes are broken in the ice and a sheet is dipped into the frigid water. Then the novice is draped in the cloth and instructed to dry it through the use of the heat generated by his body. The procedure is repeated throughout the night and, at daybreak, the dried sheets are tallied. Some dry as many as forty sheets in one night.

THE PARTY GIRL OF
RESURRECTION CEMETERY

In 1931, a young girl was killed while being driven home from a dance at the O'Henry Ballroom on Chicago's Archer Avenue. Wearing her white party dress and dancing shoes, she was buried in Resurrection Cemetery, also on the same street.

For years afterward, motorists reported seeing a beautiful young woman wearing an old-fashioned white dress and hitchhiking on Archer Avenue. Mostly single males would pick her up, or she would jump into the car uninvited, asking to be driven home. Then, she'd instruct them to drop her off at Resurrection Cemetery. Some drivers claimed she would exit the car without opening the door.

One night in December 1977, a man drove past and noticed a young woman in a long white gown standing behind the gate of Resurrection Cemetery. Thinking that perhaps she had been inadvertently locked inside, the driver called the police. But by the time they arrived, the woman had vanished. They noticed, however, that the bars of the cemetery's wrought iron gate were bent slightly outward. And on either side they could see the distinct imprints of two hands.

Edgar Cayce's Psychic Gift

Famed psychic Edgar Cayce made parapsychological history during the thirties with his medical predictions through trance channeling, engaging spiritual entities to speak through him while he remained in a sleeplike trance. Cayce said he first became aware of his considerable talents at the age of thirteen, while reading the Bible on the family farm in Hopkinsville, Kentucky. Suddenly sensing that he was not alone, he had looked up to see a woman standing in front of him. The bright sun behind her made it impossible to see her features clearly. But when she spoke, her voice was unnaturally soft and lyrical.

"Your prayers have been heard," she said, telling him that he only had to ask and she would give him anything he wanted.

What he wanted most, he replied, trembling, was to be helpful to others, especially children when they're sick. With that, the woman vanished, never to be seen again. And Edgar had the feeling that he might be losing his mind.

Cayce's teachers had always complained that the boy, never a particularly good student, was inattentive, which never pleased his father. One evening following his vision, young Edgar was struggling with his spelling lessons, with the help of his father who was determined that his son would learn to spell if it was the last thing he did. They pored over the spelling primer, with Edgar having little success. Then, he suddenly heard the same magical voice again, this time telling him, "If you can sleep a little, we can help you." Pleading with his father, he then curled up in an armchair with his schoolbook under his head.

After his nap, his lessons resumed and, to his father's amazement, Edgar not only spelled every word correctly on the first attempt, but went on to spell words in future lessons. He knew the page numbers for every lesson and could identify the illustrations accompanying them. From that point on, Edgar retained his ability to almost photographically recall material after he had literally slept on it.

It wasn't long after this that he may have performed his first psychic diagnosis—on himself. During school recess, the young Edgar was hit with a baseball, which struck him near the base of his spine. While there didn't seem to be any serious injury, the normally reserved teenager behaved strangely for the rest of the day, throwing things at his sister and sassing his father. And that night, his parents heard him talking in his sleep, saying that he was suffering from shock as a result of the injury to his spine and he prescribed the appropriate treatment: a poultice of cornmeal, onions, and herbs applied to the back of his head. Figuring it couldn't do any harm, his parents followed his mysterious advice. Sure enough, Edgar was back to normal, although he didn't remember a thing about the day before.

THE INDESTRUCTIBLE GRAVEDIGGER

Gravediggers in post–Civil War New Orleans intensely resented Samuel Dombey's low rates for opening the final resting places of the dead. So they enlisted the reputed magical powers of a Dr. Beauregard, paying fifty dollars for his "supreme curse." The next morning, as Dombey was digging in the cemetery, he heard a loud explosion and saw someone stagger from the nearby bushes. Beauregard, who was later seen heavily bandaged, apparently overloaded the gun with buckshot, causing it to blow up.

The Beauregard incident wasn't the only attempt to kill Dombey, despite the fact that the man soon seemed to be indestructible. When Beauregard obviously bungled the job, the gravediggers decided to take matters into their own hands. They first placed a keg of gunpowder under Dombey's cot in the toolshed and ignited it while he was asleep. The explosion destroyed the shed, but Dombey, thrown twenty feet, was unharmed.

Dombey's competitors, however, were not easily thwarted. Not long after the shed explosion, the gravedigger was kidnapped and, with his hands and feet bound, dropped in Lake Pontchartrain. But Dombey managed to wriggle free and make it back to shore.

Still, the attempted drowning was not the gravediggers' last effort to rid themselves of Dombey. When, next, they set fire to his house, they waited for Dombey to run outside, at which point they riddled him with buckshot. Firemen rushed to the scene and extinguished the fire, and then rushed Dombey to the hospital, where he recovered.

The gravediggers were never able to kill Indestructible Sam, as the police had begun calling Dombey. In fact, Dombey died of natural causes at the age of ninety-eight, having outlived the men who had tried to kill him.

THE FIRE ABSORBER

The firewalking display at the summer palace in Mysore, a town in southern India, was not a religious ceremony, the maharajah told Monsignor Despartures. It was simply a spectacle the Roman Catholic bishop might enjoy. Indeed, the bishop arrived early enough to observe the preparations as well as the event itself. He watched the trench being dug to a length of thirteen feet, a width of six feet, and a depth of one foot, and saw the fire lighted in the pit, giving off so much heat that the spectators would have to sit at least twenty-five feet away.

When all was prepared, the Muslim from northern India who hosted the event stood at the edge of the trench, but not in it, and called for one of the palace servants, ordering him to step into the flaming pit. When the servant refused to comply, the Muslim forced him into the fire. As the spectators watched in amazement, the servant's look of horror quickly became one of relieved surprise. Though his legs and feet were unprotected, the man was not being burned. Seeing that their colleague was unharmed, other curious servants filed, one by one, into the flames. Soon, ten of them were cavorting among the embers, all seemingly unaffected by the heat.

The servants were then followed into the fire by the maharajah's band. "The flames which rose to lick their faces bellied out round different parts of the instruments they carried, and only flickered round the sheets of music without setting them on fire," the bishop reported.

By the end of the exhibition, some two hundred people, including two visiting Englishmen, had gone into the trench, emerging unharmed. As the maharajah rose to call an end to the proceedings, however, the Muslim suddenly fell to the ground, writhing in agonizing pain. He begged for water and drank greedily. Moments later, he was back to normal. A Brahmin standing near Monsignor Despartures offered the only explanation for the incredible display, saying, "He has taken upon himself the burning of the fire."

THE FLIGHT TO NOWHERE

On December 5, 1945, five torpedo bombers took off from Fort Lauderdale, Florida, on a 320-mile navigational training exercise identified as Flight 19. The aircraft, judged to have been in perfect operational order at the time of takeoff, were manned by experienced pilots, including Lieutenant Charles Carroll Taylor, and fourteen other pilots and crews. The route should have taken them eastward, then to the north, over Grand Bahama Island, before heading southwest on their return to base, all within the area designated as the Bermuda Triangle. Instead, the maneuvers became a five-hour flight to nowhere.

Less than two hours into the flight, Taylor reported that both his compasses were inexplicably malfunctioning, and they were no longer able to determine where they were or where they were going. They assumed, for some still unknown reason, that they were somewhere over the Florida Keys, some two hundred miles off their proscribed course. Fragmentary and confusing messages continued to pepper the radio waves for another three hours before Taylor announced that they would attempt to land the planes, dangerously low on fuel, together in the water.

Despite a five-day search that covered a 250,000-mile area, during which a Martin Mariner rescue plane with a crew of 15 *also* disappeared, not a trace of the five bombers was ever found. It's likely that the airmen were unable to escape before the ditched planes sank, but not even a four-hundred-page naval inquiry could answer all the questions surrounding the bizarre circumstances leading up to the man's disappearance.

Since December 5, 1945, hundreds of large and small craft and airplanes have vanished without trace in the Bermuda Triangle. Twenty percent of these have disappeared during the first part of December, a number on December 5. But December is not within the hurricane season.

MYSTERIOUS ANIMALS

The mountains, jungles, and oceans could be home for large lizards, pygmy elephants, even Neanderthal men, as well as an array of other creatures still undiscovered. And zoologist Bernard Heuvelmans has put together a list of more than a hundred mysterious animals, documented with twenty-five thousand references, still not classified by scientists.

There is evidence that some of the strange creatures are more than mythological. There are footprints of Sasquatch and an African dragon, photos of a gigantic African snake and the Loch Ness monster, and a specimen of a Neanderthal man that was shot several decades ago in Vietnam.

Ohio State University anthropologist Frank Poirier agrees that some anomalous animals probably do exist. Others may have become extinct in modern times. It's foolish, he adds, to think there could not be new species of animals to discover.

FAINTING GOATS

In 1978, veterinarian Renfrow Hauser's father took an unusual goat to his son's Mount Airy, North Carolina, farm. Hauser took one look at the goat and it stiffened and fell over as if it were dead. It wasn't, but the animal was suffering from myotonia, a rare disease that blocks the uptake of neurotransmitters. The goat would become as stiff as a statue whenever it was startled, falling over in a dead faint.

The swooning goat was subsequently bred with nonswooners, and there was soon a community of twenty-five goats inheriting the patriarch disease, the largest known population of myotonic goats in the world. Because of their affliction the goats serve little practical purpose except as pets. The Hauser farm, moreover, is often visited by people who go just to watch the goats keel over, which they frequently do in response to low-flying planes, loud yelling, or even clapping hands. Hauser often comes upon them while driving his pickup truck and when he blows the horn to get them out of the road, they just fall over in a ditch. The more contact the goats have with humans, however, the less likely they are to faint.

THE PHANTOM BATTLE OF BÜDERICH

The government of Westphalia collected no less than fifty eyewitness reports of a phantom battle that took place on January 22, 1854, in the village of Büderich. According to the observers, the entire army—infantry, cavalry, and numerous wagons—marched in procession across the countryside. The discharges from the rifles and the color of the uniforms could be clearly seen, and as the battalion headed toward the wood of Schafhauser, they left in their wake two burning houses and a trail of thick, black smoke. Then the army disappeared into the forest.

At sunset, the entire scene dissipated, as suddenly and inexplicably as it had appeared.

THE LITTLE TOWN OF BETHSAIDA

The fishing village of Bethsaida is said to have been the hometown of the apostles Peter, Andrew, and Philip, as well as the locale where Jesus performed some of his greatest miracles. It is from Bethsaida's shores that he walked on the Sea of Galilee, and where he healed a blind man and fed five thousand people with the transformation of five loaves of bread and two fishes. Herod the Great's son, Herod Philip, elevated Bethsaida's status to that of a city because of its large population. But despite historical references to the city, nobody has ever been able to find it.

As early as A.D. 530, scholars disagreed on the location of Bethsaida. By the nineteenth century, researchers had pinned down two possible sites—one near the mouth of the Jordan River, and the other et-Tell, the largest mound on the northern coast of the Sea of Galilee. Now, archaeologist Rami Arav believes he has found the remains of Bethsaida about four feet beneath the eighty-foot-high et-Tell.

The town beneath et-Tell, Arav says, dates back to about the third century B.C. For some reason, the site was abandoned suddenly, probably around A.D. 70 during the war between the Jews and the Romans.

THE MYSTERY OF MARTIN BORMANN

Much speculation surrounds the fate of Martin Bormann, the trusted aide and confidant of Adolph Hitler. Reports place him at Hitler's side when the Führer and Eva Braun committed suicide in a bunker outside Berlin on April 30, 1945. After disposing of the bodies according to Hitler's own instructions, Bormann allegedly left with the rest of Hitler's staff in a convoy of tanks. But after that evening, Bormann officially became a missing person, sentenced to death *in absentia* by the Nuremburg war crimes tribunal.

Rumors continue to circulate, however. According to one popular theory at the time, Bormann was killed in Denmark while attempting to contact Hitler's successor, Admiral Karl Doenitz. Others had him escaping through the Alps to Italy, or via submarine to South America. As late as 1973, he was said to have been seen in a Bolivian hospital.

REVENGE OF THE CACTUS

In 1982, David Grundman aimed his gun and fired two shots at a giant saguaro cactus in the desert outside Phoenix, Arizona. The blasts caused a twenty-three-foot section of the cactus to fall over, landing on Grundman and crushing him to death.

THE LOCH NESS BUSH MONSTER

Cryptozoologists, who search for proof of creatures considered to be mythological, have generally assumed that the Loch Ness monster, known endearingly as Nessie, is strictly a marine animal. But on at least two occasions, Nessie apparently left the confines of the Scottish lake and walked on dry land.

In the summer of 1933, George Spicer and his wife, of Inverness, Scotland, were enjoying a leisurely vacation drive to the little town of Foyers. Suddenly, they noticed movement in the brush along the side of the road near Loch Ness. Slowing down to a full stop, they saw a huge, long-necked animal emerge from its roadside cover. It was at least six feet long and four feet high. Spicer described it as "a terrible, dark elephant gray, of a loathsome texture, reminiscent of a snail." It proceeded to lumber across the road and vanished in the bushes on the opposite side, returning, they suspected, to the lake.

Less than six months later, medical student Arthur Grant was riding his motorcycle on a moonlit road near Lochend when he also sighted a huge dark shape in the roadside bushes. Grant estimated its length to be about eighteen to twenty feet long. The creature had an elongated neck and tail, and was eel-like, with oval eyes. And the four legs resembled flippers, definitely not designed for walking. The animal was bulky and awkward, so Grant thought he'd be able to catch it. But it was faster than he'd imagined.

Grant did manage to get a good look at the walking lake monster, however, and drew a detailed illustration when he returned home. According to Grant, it appeared to be either a prehistoric plesiosaur or a giant seal.

PAINTED ARSON

The Crying Boy, a popular painting sold in British stores, depicts an angel-faced child with a tear perched on his plump, rosy cheek. But the portrait may not be as innocent as the child appears, according to a retired Yorkshire, England, fireman.

It first struck Alan Wilkinson that something was curious about the painting when it was found, undamaged, in the rubble of a thoroughly destructive house fire. In the years following that first incident, Wilkinson compiled fifty similar accounts in Yorkshire alone. A typical case would take place in a house almost completely gutted by fire. Pictures in every other room would be destroyed by the flames, but *The Crying Boy* would be found without so much as a smudge. As the story of *The Crying Boy* was spread by local newspapers, there was speculation that the painting was actually responsible for the fires in which it was involved.

Some owners of the painting, convinced that it was jinxed, removed it from their homes. One woman took her copy directly to Wilkinson and asked him to destroy it for her. Wilkinson left it in the fire station office, and the same day a kitchen oven overheated and burned all the firefighters' dinners.

ROSES FROM NOWHERE

Russian mystic and medium Madame Blavatsky had a magnetic personality. On one particular night in India, for example, she was in the company of several Indian scholars, a German professor of Sanskrit, and her devoted disciple Colonel Olcott. At one point in the evening, the German professor remarked that ancient Indian sages were supposedly able to perform miracles, amazing feats like making roses fall out of the sky. Those days were gone, he lamented. No one had such powers any longer.

Madame Blavatsky took up the challenge, berating modern Hindus for not emulating their ancestors more. But she would prove that such feats as pulling roses out of nowhere could still be done—and by a Western woman, too.

She pressed her lips together tightly and grandly swept her right hand. And with that, one dozen roses cascaded down from out of nowhere. Without another comment, Madame Blavatsky then resumed her previous conversation.

INCREDIBLE MONSTERS THAT FLY

Many cultures possess stories of otherworldly creatures that fly, chief of which is probably the flying, fire-breathing dragon. Among others, however, there are the Greeks' winged Harpies and the Native American thunderbird. There are fossil remains, of course, for what could be the precursor of all flying monsters: the prehistoric pterodactyl, a sharp-toothed reptile with a wingspan of more than twenty-five feet. But there have been reports that such creatures may be a present day reality.

There have been occasional reports of the "Jersey Devil" being sighted in New Jersey. The creature is said to be the size of a large crane, and described as having a long, thick neck, long hind legs, short forelegs, a wingspan of two feet, the head of a horse, or dog, or ram, and a long tail.

A frightening creature called the Kongamato resembles a flying lizard with smooth skin, a beak full of teeth, and batlike wings stretching four to seven feet when fully spread. And the Mothman, a man-shaped, winged creature that instills bone-chilling fear, has been sighted throughout the United States, from Texas to West Virginia.

WINDS THAT ROCK THE EARTH

Blustery March winds may be strong enough to knock you off your feet, but it would seem that, no matter how strong, wind couldn't possibly trigger earthquakes. Even so, Jerome Namias of the Scripps Institute of Oceanography in La Jolla, California, has studied high-pressure systems, which often spawn high winds. And two such occurrences may have been responsible for the earthquakes that rocked southern California in July and October 1987. During the six-week to month-long period prior to the quakes, Namias found a recurring series of high-pressure systems over the Pacific Ocean several hundred miles off the West Coast of the United States. Their unusual strength, he speculates, could exert pressure on the ocean floor, which in turn adds stress to the inland fault lines along California's geography

Namias points out that other research has demonstrated that the force exerted on mountain ranges by global wind systems can alter the rate of the earth's rotation. Therefore, it is not unreasonable that winds may at times also cause earthquakes.

The Worst Nightmare

In 1924, attorney Thornton Jones dreamed that he committed suicide. He awoke with a start, and realized that he had slit his own throat. Motioning to his wife for pencil and paper, he wrote, "I dreamt that I had done it. I awoke to find it true." He died about an hour later.

Biting Poltergeists

Thirteen-year-old Molly Giles and her younger sister were taken to the local pharmacist by their distraught parents. Beyond the girls' stating that "something" had bitten them, no one could explain the savage bite marks covering the girls' arms. According to the Ghost Research Society founder, Martin Riccardo, however, Molly and her sister had encountered a biting poltergeist.

According to Riccardo, who has documented at least half a dozen cases involving vicious ghosts, biting poltergeists is a rare phenomenon but, nonetheless, a horrible experience. In 1922, for example, the National Laboratory of Psychical Research examined Eleonora Zugon, a thirteen-year-old Romanian girl who had been bitten on the back and neck by some unseen attacker. While shocked researchers looked on, moreover, more teethmarks appeared on her flesh for no apparent reason.

Witnesses also observed eighteen-year-old Clarita Villanueva struggling with an invisible assailant in a Philippines police station in 1953. What they initially thought was a seizure turned out to be otherwise. When the attack subsided, Clarita's arms and legs were covered with bloody bite marks.

THE SEARCH FOR EL DORADO

In 1492 when Christopher Columbus discovered the first of many Caribbean islands, he was on a journey to find a new route to the Orient, in search of spices, jewels, gold, and silver. He found none of them, and before long Europe was losing the hope of unearthing great riches in the New World. In 1520, however, interest quickly blossomed again when Hernán Cortés returned with the treasures bestowed on him by the last Aztec Emperor Montezuma: a finely worked duck, ornaments in the shape of human figures, ear plugs, chihuahuas, statues of tigers, panthers, and monkeys, all in gold and objects that dazzled the Europeans. It was the hint of El Dorado, *el hombre dorado*, the man of gold. And the quest to find him has carried into the twentieth century.

Ten years later after Cortés spread out the Mexican riches before the Spanish monarchs, Charles I of Spain appointed German banker Ambrosius Dalfinger the first governor of

Venezuela. Dalfinger arrived and almost immediately set out to explore the territory. Reaching Lake Maracaibo, he found gold and legends of gold. The golden ornaments and objects were abundant. The gold, they told Dalfinger, came from a people further in the interior, a people so rich their ruler, El Dorado, painted himself gold. After repeated attempts, however, Dalfinger died in the jungle without finding El Dorado. But he had acquired another clue: The gold, he was told, came from the same place as the salt did.

The desire to find El Dorado mounted. Dalfinger's successor, Georg Hohermuth, among others, also searched for El Dorado—unsuccessfully, although without realizing it, he had come within less than a hundred miles of what might have been their goal, later found by Gonzalo Jiménez de Quesada. At the southern border of the land dominated by the Chibcha Indians, salt was profusely abundant. Here, Queseda's men tortured some of the Indians to reveal the source of their emeralds, which they then traded for gold as the expedition continued.

Then in June 1536, Quesada was led to Hunsa whose villagers were ladened with gold. There was even a real El Dorado: The chibcha's coronation ceremony includes the new king being anointed with sap and covered with gold dust. Even so, Quesada himself didn't believe he had found the city of El Dorado, and his discovery did nothing to stem the search. Even Sir Walter Raleigh made two attempts at finding it.

Two or three times every century, someone has gone off in search of El Dorado. In the early part of this century, Colonel Percy Fawcett became the successor to the adventurous seekers, disappearing around 1920, presumably in the dense frontier of Brazil and Bolivia. More important than how he died is the question of whether Fawcett found what he was looking for. If El Dorado does exist and hasn't actually been found, it still awaits another person of sufficient action and daring to attempt it.

KAMIKAZE BIRDS

Suicide is almost unheard of in the animal kingdom, but in a freakish display, four hundred robins perished when they flew, en masse, straight into a concrete wall. Some cats pursuing the dead or dying birds were then killed by late-coming dive-bombing kamikaze birds. On the adjoining Highway 101 near Mountain View, California, a multicar wreck resulted when drivers attempted to avoid the mess.

Karen Fraad, of the Santa Clara County Humane Society, doesn't believe the suicide was instinctive, or even planned. The robins, she suggests, were drunk. It seems that alongside Highway 101, the California Department of Transportation had planted pyracantha bushes, its fermented berries known to intoxicate birds. The robins had feasted on the alcoholic berries, Fraad speculates, and they became disoriented. Not knowing where they were going, the birds began to fly low. The wall, Fraad points out, just happened to be in their way.

In response to Fraad's protests about the heady plants, the California Department of Transportation has, for the most part, removed and replaced the pyracantha bushes.

Death by Insomnia

A middle-aged Italian industrial manager suddenly developed insomnia, which grew worse as it continued to plague the man and responded to no known medical treatment. By the third month of the illness, he slept for only one hour a night and that was disturbed by vivid dreams that made him rise from his bed and give a military salute. Other symptoms included impotence, amnesia, and an incurable lung infection. Within a year of the insomnia's onset, he died from total exhaustion.

When neuropathologists autopsied the insomniac's brain, they found a lesion on the thalamus as well as 85 to 95 percent of the neurons destroyed in two parts of the region. The doctors learned that four other relatives had been similarly affected, including a sister whose autopsied brain indicated she had died from the same strange, unidentified malady.

THE GREEN CHILDREN OF BANJOS

The villagers of Banjos, Spain, were visited by a mysterious twosome in August 1887. The young boy and girl emerged from a nearby mountain cave. Their skin was green, the shape of their eyes appeared Asian, and they wore clothing made of an unidentifiable material, and neither spoke Spanish. The boy died shortly afterward, but the girl eventually learned enough Spanish to explain her extraordinary origins: The children had come from a land where there was no sun, she said. One day, a great whirlwind had carried her and her companion away, depositing them in the Banjos cave. The investigators were still baffled five years later when the girl died.

THE PRESERVED COAL MINER

In 1869, miners found the body of a young man in the airless Fort Smith, Arkansas, coal pits. It caused a stir in the community, and a crowd had quickly gathered to see who the man might be. When the miners brought the perfectly preserved corpse to the surface, a gray-haired old woman slipped past the crowd and threw herself on the youthful corpse, crying and pouring out a stream of endearments. She and the dead miner, it turned out, were to have been married the day after his disappearance forty years earlier.

THE BANSHEE OF COUNTY MONAGHAN

Gaelic banshees are a most benevolent sort of spirit. These female guardian ghosts will attach themselves to an individual or family for life, and foretell the imminent death of their wards by shrieking and wailing. One of the best known was the Rossmore banshee of County Monaghan, Ireland, and her cry was first heard in 1801, at the death of General Robert Cunningham, the first Baron Rossmore.

During a stay at Cunningham's home, Sir Jonah and Lady Barrington retired early, proposing to rise early. At two in the morning, however, they were awakened from a deep sleep by a piercing wail. The voice began to clearly and repeatedly scream the name Rossmore, continuing for a half hour. When the crying finally ceased, Sir Jonah and Lady Barrington went back to sleep, still bewildered and shaken by the disturbance.

When they rose later, they discovered that their host, the Baron Rossmore, had died in his sleep at about two-thirty that morning.

ON A TRAIN TO NOWHERE

In September 1890, Louis Le Prince's future looked bright. Having demonstrated his process for making motion pictures at the Paris Opéra, he would have received the accolades for a technique later reinvented by Thomas Edison. But the last time anyone saw him, he was boarding a train in Paris. Seven years later he was declared legally dead.

RETURN OF THE EXTINCT
TASMANIAN TIGER

The last known living Tasmanian tiger, also known as the Tasmanian wolf, or thylacine, was captured in Tasmania in 1933 and died in a zoo in 1936. Although the animal was believed to have become extinct on the mainland of Australia a thousand years ago, sightings have been reported during the last fifty-five years. And in the eighties, the Australian government hired Kevin Cameron, an experienced Australian aborigine tracker, to investigate the reports.

In the past, sightings have stirred numerous searches, but

there has never been any proof that the creature existed. And even though Cameron later reported seeing at least four separate Tasmanian tigers in the dense forest, each displaying the animal's characteristic weaving gait, the authorities remained skeptical. So Cameron went back for more concrete evidence, this time producing photographs of an animal about the size of a dog, with dark stripes across its hind end, another distinct characteristic of the tiger. He also obtained casts of footprints—very clear forefeet with five toes and hindfeet with only four. Despite accepted scientific knowledge, some researchers believe Cameron's sightings are authentic. And Athol Douglas, retired experimental officer at the Western Australian Museum in Perth, estimates that there are at least six Tasmanian tigers living in the Australian forest.

VANISHING INTO THIN AIR

It's one thing to disappear without a trace, but to do it in front of witnesses is bizarre, to say the least. Even so, that is exactly what happened to Orion Williamson in July 1854 before the very eyes of his wife, daughter, and two neighbors in Selma, Alabama. One moment, he was walking across his pasture; the next he was gone. And a subsequent search that included the use of bloodhounds revealed no hidden holes and no sign of Williamson.

A similar incident took place in September 1880, in Gallatin, Tennessee, when farmer David Lang took off on a tour of his fields, in full view of his wife, and simply vanished into thin air. The disappearance was also witnessed by August Peck, a local judge, and his brother-in-law who had arrived at the Lang farm just moments before and had waved at the farmer.

Mysterious evidence in other similar cases includes footprints that continue for a while and then suddenly stop. One night in November 1878, for example, sixteen-year-old Charles Ashmore of Quincy, Indiana, went on a simple water-gathering errand and never returned. When they went out searching for him later, Charles's father and sister found and followed his fresh tracks in the damp soil, but they ended suddenly less than halfway to the well.

In two oddly coincidental cases, also involving wells, eleven-year-old boys, both named Oliver, disappeared on Christmas Eve, although ten years apart and on two different continents. Oliver Larch disappeared in 1889 on his way to the family well in South Bend, Indiana. Oliver Thomas of Rhayader, Wales, seems to have fallen victim to mysterious forces in 1909: His family heard his anguished cries of "Help! They've got me!" But when they rushed outdoors, the boy was nowhere around. They followed his footprints until they abruptly ended halfway to the well.

BIBLICAL AIDS

Sexually transmitted diseases have been reported since the beginning of medical history, but the AIDS epidemic, some believe, is uniquely new. British chemist John Gwilt, vice president of the New York-based Sterling Drug Company, however, argues that there is evidence in the Bible that ancient Israelites suffered from an eerily similar affliction.

According to Gwilt, the twenty-fifth chapter of the Bible's book of Numbers recounts an encounter between the Israelites and the Moabite religious prostitutes. Their intermingling resulted in the illness and subsequent death of twenty-four thousand Israelites. Although Gwilt believes that figure may have been an error in translation—he estimates the death toll was probably twenty-four hundred—these sexual encounters of the Israelites had very definite deadly consequences.

The Bible, in fact, is full of medical descriptions, from heart attacks and hypothermia to epilepsy and sudden infant death syndrome, that are surprisingly accurate in terms of modern medical knowledge. The Old Testament, moreover, contains references to diseases not yet known to man. In Zechariah, Gwilt points out as an example, it's written that "Their flesh shall rot while they stand on their feet, their eyes shall rot in their sockets, and their tongues shall rot in their mouths." It seems to describe exactly what would happen to people in the event of a nuclear meltdown or holocaust.

DEATH AT THE THIRTEENTH HOLE

Michael Scaglione was playing golf with friends on April 25, 1982, in New Orleans, when he made a bad shot on the thirteenth hole. He became so angry with himself that he threw his club against the golf cart with such force that the club broke, the club head rebounding and stabbing Scaglione in the throat, severing his jugular vein. Staggering, Scaglione pulled the piece of metal from his neck. But he died from the rapid flow of blood.

ESCAPE OF THE GIANT SQUID

The weather was perfect, and although there was a silent swell, the ocean was calm for miles around. So when the crew of the French sloop *Alecton* first sighted the monstrous sea creature on November 30, 1861, they were quite certain that it wasn't a wave or even a rock. It was, they later recounted, the legendary giant squid whose existence had been long disputed.

Sighted as the *Alecton* sailed from Cadiz, Spain, to Tenerife, the giant squid was approximately eighteen feet long, with eight limbs and a huge tail. Lieutenant Bouyer, the *Alecton*'s commander, described it as "quite appalling, brick red in color, shapeless, and slimy, its form repulsive and terrible."

Even so, the commander set out to capture the beast, but the pitching of the vessel made it impossible for crew members to shoot it. When they were finally able to harpoon the squid, and even snag its tail in a noose, they realized the creature was stronger than they had imagined. Waving its tentacles and rearing a head with a curious parrotlike beak, the giant squid broke free of the ropes, leaving a forty-pound portion of its tail behind.

GEOGLYPHIC DESIGNS
VISIBLE ONLY FROM THE SKY

About ten thousand years ago, prehistoric residents of Native American origin built vast stone alignments in present-day Panamint valley in southeastern California. But the birds, snakes, and geometrical designs of overlapping hoops and parallel lines are recognizable only from the air. Some of the approximately sixty alignments are as long as a football field; others cover only sixteen or seventeen feet. And as many as seven hundred stones about six inches high were used in the designs.

The real enigma is why hunter-gatherers would build them in such a dry, remote location, particularly when the geoglyphics could never be seen by the designers of Native American origin. Or could they? The alignments, as in the case of the Nazca Lines in Peru, could be a form of astronomy, or they may have had some religious or magical significance.

THE DRUNK WHO WOULD
NOT DIE

In 1933, Anthony Marino and four friends, experiencing financial problems, carried out an ingenious, although diabolical plan: They murdered Marino's girlfriend in order to collect on her life insurance policy. Since the scam had worked so well, they decided to try it again, setting their sights on Michael Malloy, an alcoholic who patronized Marino's speakeasy in the Bronx. Having taken out three insurance policies in his name, the idea was to kill him in such a way that no one would ever suspect foul play, but Malloy proved to be a difficult victim to murder.

Thinking that Malloy, given the opportunity, would drink himself to death, Marino gave him unlimited credit at the bar. When Malloy continued to drink without even keeling over, however, the bartender, who was a partner in the scam, replaced the liquor with antifreeze. Although Malloy did finally pass out, he came to a few hours later and began drinking again, guzzling antifreeze for another week.

The bartender began filling Malloy with turpentine, and then horse liniment laced with rat poison. Yet Malloy kept returning for more. They fed him rotten oysters drenched in wood alcohol and spoiled sardines mixed with carpet tacks and Malloy would ask for second helpings. They dumped him in the snow and watered him down, leaving him to weather the night in temperatures that dropped to minus fourteen degrees Fahrenheit. But nothing would kill Michael Malloy.

Finally they hired a professional killer who, driving a car at forty-five miles per hour, struck Malloy, hurling him into the air and then running over him. After three weeks in the hospital, however, Malloy returned to the speakeasy and resumed drinking.

Finally they connected a rubber hose to a gas jet and forced the opposite end up Malloy's nose, leaving it there until his face turned purple. They succeeded in killing the man, but in the long run still failed because the authorities discovered their crime. They were arrested and sentenced to the electric chair.

CHAMP: THE MONSTER
INHABITING LAKE CHAMPLAIN

Lake Champlain is a tranquil hundred-mile-long body of water linking Vermont and New York with Canada. Beneath it, however, may lurk an extraordinary marine monster. Some of the first people to sight it were six people on a pleasure cruise in the lake on August 30, 1878. It had two large folds at the back of its head that had projected above the water. Another pair of folds appeared about fifty feet behind, presumably at the tail end.

Dubbed Champ, the creature has been sighted at various times since. In 1971, for example, Mrs. Robert Green, her mother, and a friend were staying at a hotel overlooking Lake Champlain when they saw a snakelike creature with three humps moving smoothly through the water. On the basis of descriptions and the nature of its habitat, there is speculation that Champ may be a distant relative of Nessie, or the Loch Ness Monster.

THE MISSING JUDGE

From 1790 to 1801, John Lansing sat on the New York State Supreme Court, serving as chief justice in 1798. A veteran of the American Revolution, he had served as a legislator and had also been the mayor of Albany, as well as state chancellor. In 1804, Lansing retired, keeping himself occupied by his involvement as a business consultant to New York's Columbia College.

On December 12, 1829, Lansing was staying in a Manhattan hotel following a meeting with Columbia College officials. After writing some letters that evening, he went out to mail them. The seventy-five-year-old statesman was never seen or heard of again, despite a comprehensive search.

ACUPUNCTURED CORN

The Chinese use the ancient medical art of acupuncture for more than correcting physical ills. They use it to also ripen corn more quickly and to improve its taste. Intrigued by the idea, Sandy, Oregon, agricultural writer Jude Ramsey Jensen decided to test the procedure, using toothpicks instead of the long, thin metal needles traditionally used on humans.

In a controlled experiment, Jensen inserted a toothpick through the base of each ear stem into the main stalk when the silk was still green. She left alternate rows of corn untouched. To her amazement, the acupunctured plants matured a full week earlier and tasted measurably sweeter than those that had not received the acupuncture treatment.

The procedure works by wounding the plant, which in turn sends healing sugars rushing to the injured area. The technique is a fine example of the logic of simplicity—the plant must deal with the wound—argues Jensen who has continued to use acupuncture on her corn. And she grows the sweetest and fastest-maturing corn in Oregon.

THE GREAT GHOSTMAKER

John Henry Pepper was an analytical chemist who became director of London's Royal Polytechnic Institute in 1852. But throughout a Victorian England equally enchanted by spiritualism as it was by science, Pepper was also known as the creator of the Ghost Show.

The Ghost Show delighted audiences by presenting eerie images that interacted with live actors on stage. The "ghost" was actually a player below the stage. From his concealed location, a projectionist illuminated the actor, reflecting his image from a mirror on to a large pane of glass, also unseen by spectators. What appeared on stage were airy apparitions that seemed to menace actors and patrons alike.

Famed as a preeminent showman of science throughout Australia, Canada, and the United States, as well as his native Great Britain, Pepper never claimed his ghosts were anything but illusions, something that was in stark contrast to the fraudulent but common practice at the time of presenting ghosts as entities that could be summoned by those who knew how to call them.

OTHERWORLD JOURNEYS
THROUGH THE AGES

As they lay dying, ancient soldiers may have seen dead relatives beckoning them toward dark tunnels leading into light. Medieval Christians probably used visions of the netherworld images to reinforce images of heaven and hell. And Virgil, Dante, and writers of epic underworld journeys may have based their heroes' stories on the out-of-body experiences of real-life people.

Such are a few of the possibilities posed in *Otherworld Journeys*, a scholarly book that analyzes near-death experiences (NDE) from ancient through modern times. Whether science or mythology, NDEs are evidence that the soul exists apart from the body. And according to the author, Harvard University professor of religion Carol Zaleski, historical insight is the key to understanding NDEs.

Astronomy, biology, and other scientific fields have progressed immeasurably during the last fifteen hundred years, but many aspects of the NDE are perennial: the soldier that returns from the dead in the sixth century and describes a footbridge where wicked souls fall into the slimy river below, while the blessed pass over to a peaceful meadow on the other side. Twentieth-century NDE guru Raymond Moody says that his subjects, too, often return to their bodies with sensations of peace.

Is There More Than One "Monster" in Loch Ness?

Over the years, there have been numerous scientific and quasi-scientific attempts to prove the existence of the Loch Ness monster. One of the most elaborate efforts was undertaken by Robert Rines for the Academy of Applied Science in 1972. His results were doubly surprising.

With sophisticated sonar equipment and a camera strobe light system, Rines and his team staked out the loch locations where "Nessie" had been most often sighted. The objective was to capture a combination of sonar and photographic evidence of Nessie.

On the night of August 8, they sat in boats anchored in Urquhart Bay a short distance from the shore. They positioned the sonar equipment on an underwater slope and the camera slightly lower and aimed at the area detected by the sonar. Then, they waited.

Around one o'clock in the morning, the sonar beam picked up a large object moving in camera range. About forty minutes later two objects appeared on the sonar screen, which the camera photographed.

Although the water was cloudy and the photographs were, therefore, vague, several astounding computer enhancements revealed not one but two possible Nessies. Analysis of the images of flippers in some photos estimates the appendages' length to be four to six feet. And the two large creatures were apparently about twelve feet apart. Rines and his team had finally produced evidence of the Loch Ness monster, but still not enough to convince skeptics.

Encouraged by the success of the 1972 expedition to Loch Ness, which produced the sonar and photographic evidence of two Nessies, the Academy of Applied Science launched another search in 1975. This time, investigators used even more sophisticated, sensitive equipment, designed to reduce the technical problems that hindered the quality of the 1972 photos. Still, the more advanced camera was unable to pick up anything except the silt stirred up by the creature that eventually appeared. Fortunately, the camera used in 1972 had also been set up as an auxiliary and recorded some remarkable images during the twenty-four-hour period on June 19 and 20: the upper torso, extended neck, stubby appendages, and the dragonlike head of a massive marine creature. Extensive examination of the photographs provided significant insight into Nessie's appearance. The overall length was twenty feet. Its neck was about eighteen inches thick, its mouth nine inches long and five inches wide, and two six-inch, horned appendages, ten inches apart, protruded from the beast's head.

These and subsequent photo images of the Nessie bear a remarkable resemblance to the plesiosaur, a prehistoric water reptile presumed extinct for more than seventy million years. The Loch Ness monster is particularly similar to one type of the plesiosaur, the elasmosaur.

SEA MONSTERS OF THE
SOVIET UNION

On a five-month expedition to survey mineral deposits in eastern Siberia in 1964, a team of Moscow University scientists set up camp near the shore of Lake Khaiyr. When one of the group, biologist N. Gladkikh, went to draw water from the lake he quite literally ran into the creature long reputed to abide there.

Scientists, of course, had always considered Lake Khaiyr's resident monster nothing more than a myth. But here was a reputable biologist, face to face with an animal the likes of which he had never seen. Its small head rested atop a long, gleaming neck connected to a huge jet-black body with a vertical fin affixed along the spine. Alarmed, Gladkikh rushed back to the campsite, returning with the other scientists and their cameras and guns. By that time, however, the creature had returned to the depths.

But a few days later, the beast reappeared, this time in full view of the entire Moscow University group. According to deputy team leader G. Rokosuev, "The creature beat the water with its long tail, producing waves on the lake." They could no longer claim the Lake Khaiyr monster was a myth.

THE GUIDING SPIRIT AT THE SOUTH POLE

The idea that spirits might guide humans is not new, but some students of spiritual lore believe such companion or counselor ghosts may have played a role in some of mankind's greatest adventures. Explorer Ernest Shackleton, for example, leading a brutal three-man trek across the Antarctic mountains in 1917, wrote that it often seemed there were four rather than three men in the group. His two colleagues during the thirty-six-hour journey concurred with the sensation of having a guiding force accompanying them.

And the spectral companion provided some very real support during the grueling expedition.

A PSYCHIC DAY AT THE RACES

While it may be true that no one has gotten rich by using ESP to bet on horse races, there have been a great many reported cases of minor, isolated successes at the track achieved with the help of psychic abilities. Some of the best reports were collected during the thirties by Dame Edith Lyttelton, a British delegate to the League of Nations with a fondness for psychical investigations.

In response to a 1934 British Broadcasting Corporation radio broadcast on the subject of precognition, listeners sent Lyttelton a flood of mail describing their own experiences with premonitions. W. L. Freeman of North Leicester, England, for example, claimed that he had not been particularly interested in horse racing, but in November of 1913, he had had a strange dream in which he was visiting a cathedral in Lincoln. Suddenly realizing the time, he ran over to the racetrack, fearing he had spent so much time in the church that he had missed the Lincoln Handicap. Someone at the track informed him that the race was indeed over and that the winning horse was named Outran. The following March, Freeman learned that one of the horses scheduled to run the 1914 Lincoln Handicap was named Outran, and despite unfavorable odds, the horse won the race.

Other cases reported to Lyttelton included an account by Phyllis Richards of London. On her way to the 1933 Grand

National race in Liverpool, Richards had dreamed that the winning horse's name began with the letter *K* and ended with "jack." The horse, however, was not the first one to cross the finish line. The winner of the actual race that day, it turned out, was Kellesboro Jack, which came in second, preceded by a riderless horse, which was disqualified.

Another premonition was experienced by a woman while she was awake, a week before the 1932 Derby. She heard a voice distinctly tell her that April the Fifth would win the race. She took a gamble and placed a small bet on the horse to win and, as she and her family then listened to the race on the radio, April the Fifth took the lead halfway through and went on to win. "A most peculiar feeling almost made me faint," the woman recalled. "Almost immediately, I burst into tears."

COMPETING PATRIOTS

John Adams, the second president of the United States, and Thomas Jefferson, the country's third president, took up a spirited, if competitive friendship when the two worked together to frame the Declaration of Independence. But it was in death that the two patriots revealed an odd coincidence. Both men died on the fiftieth anniversary of the Declaration's signing, July 4, 1826. Even more curious, they seemed to have willed themselves to live until that date, partly out of a sense of patriotism, but more because neither wanted the other to die first.

On his deathbed in Virginia, in fact, Jefferson asked for confirmation of the date before expiring, while a hundred miles away in New England, Adams uttered his famous last words: "Thomas Jefferson still lives." Adams ultimately outlived Jefferson by five hours.

THE BEAST OF EXMOOR

The legendary Beast of Exmoor is said to roam the moors and hills of western England, killing hundreds of sheep and stalking unwary travelers. But naturalist Trevor Beer is certain that the creature is no myth. He has, in fact, even managed to photograph the black catlike beast while it ravaged rabbits on a hillside.

Beer leads guided tours through the beast's habitat for the Kittiwell Hotel, which provides a unique package to curious tourists. (With the price of a four-day weekend, guests receive full board and a chance to glimpse the Beast-of-Exmoor). But how does Beer explain the beast's presence in the English countryside? "I think that over the years, big cats have escaped from circuses and exotic pet situations," he explains. "Now we have a feral breeding population in the British Isles."

Beer believes there is actually more than one Beast of Exmoor and, he says, the beasts are perfectly harmless. He wants to make sure, moreover, that the creature is protected. He gives the tours to attract attention and sympathy for the cats.

THE TINY TUNNELS OF
ANCIENT MEXICO

The Zapotec Indians flourished in southwest Mexico from 200 B.C. until the Spanish invasion in 1519. Like the Olmecs and the Maya before them, the Zapotecs had a highly developed civilization, skilled in the fields of art, astronomy, and architecture. Their origins, however, are unknown, although according to Indian myth, the Zapotecs believed they were descended from trees, rocks, and jaguars. But this is not the question unanswered about the Zapotec civilization.

The remains of the Zapotec capital, known today as Monte Albán, lie seven miles from the modern Mexican city of Oaxaca, atop an artificially leveled mountain. The ancient city is flanked on all sides by terraced steps, sunken courtyards, and low-rising buildings. Archaeologists excavating the site in 1931 were impressed by the gold, jade, and turquoise they found in abundance in the tombs of Zapotec leaders. But the most amazing discovery was a complex network of tiny tunnels, far too small to be used by adults or even average-sized children.

The tunnels' dimensions range from twenty inches high by twenty-five inches wide to even smaller ones no more than a foot high. At first, archaeologists thought the passageways were some sort of underground drainage system. But when excavators actually entered the tunnels, with great difficulty—they could make their way through them only by lying on their backs and pulling themselves along—they found human skeletons at the end of each one, and around the bones, the same sort of riches they had found in the tombs.

The purpose of the pygmy tunnels of Monte Albán remains unexplained.

UNLUCKY LUCKY NUMBER

People who regularly play the horses or the lottery often seek to bet on their lucky number: their birthdate, address, or license plate number, for example. One day in 1958, however, thousands of New Yorkers chose a most unlucky number, one that turned out to have a remarkable change of fortune.

A Jersey Central railroad train plummeted from a trestle bridge into Newark Bay below. News photographers and cameramen rushed to the scene and captured a shot of the rear car as it was being lifted by crane out of the water. The following day, the picture appeared on the front page of at least one newspaper. Clearly visible on the side of the raised car was the number 932.

That same day, not only had thousands of New Yorkers placed their money on 932 in the numbers game and won, but the winning lottery number was also 932.

CANINE GHOSTS

For more than forty years, Ballechin House in Perthshire, Scotland, had been the home of Major Stewart, an eccentric man with a penchant for spiritualism and a great fondness for dogs. At the time of his death in 1876, he owned fourteen dogs, all living in Ballechin House. Not knowing what to do with them when the major died, unthinking relatives had all of them put to sleep. One afternoon not long after the dogs' extermination, the wife of the major's nephew was in the Ballechin study when she detected the unmistakable odor of dogs. Suddenly, she felt a push, feeling oddly like a dog's nudge. And so began Ballechin's reputation as a haunted house.

After the nephew's death in a London car accident, Ballechin House passed into the hands of a relative named Captain Stewart, who proceeded to successfully rent the estate to people wishing to use the grounds for sport hunting, despite the house's reputation. But in August 1896, so disturbed by horrible sounds in the night and mysterious nudges at their legs, the occupants forfeited their money and fled.

Soon, the house came to the attention of the Marquis of Bute, a member of the Psychical Research Society. The Marquis and his colleagues decided to have a party at Ballechin House, by way of investigating the canine ghosts. During the course of the festivities, the thirty-five guests heard bizarre sounds, muffled explosions, shuffling feet, and someone interminably reading aloud, which they initially attributed to owls in the attic and faulty water pipes. They later began accusing each other of fabricating the sounds. But when something began pounding on the door and a number of persons perceived a misty figure resembling a spaniel, the Marquis and his guests realized that some strong spiritual force was indeed at work in Ballechin House.

THE TIE THAT BINDS
BROTHERS

George and Hart Northey were exceptionally close during their childhood and had never been apart for any length of time. But when George, the elder of the two brothers, joined the navy, Hart remained at home in St. Eglos, Cornwall, England, where he entered the family business.

One night in February 1840, while his ship was docked at the port in St. Helena, George had a strange and disturbing dream. In it, he quite vividly saw himself at his brother's side as Hart worked in the marketplace in Trebodwina, a town not far from St. Eglos. Every detail, every action, was precise and clear, so much so that George believed he had traveled the miles and was actually at his brother's side. He had been unable to communicate with Hart in the dream, however; he could only accompany him and observe.

George's dream had begun with Hart journeying home with the day's receipts. As he neared the village of Polkerrow, he was accosted by two men, familiar to George as notorious poachers. While the helpless George looked on, the two villains robbed Hart at gunpoint and fatally shot him. Setting Hart's horse loose, they dragged the corpse to a nearby stream. Then the murderers covered all traces of blood on the road and hid the pistol in the thatch of an empty hut. On waking, George was filled with such dread that during the entire trip home from St. Helena the next day, he fretted that his dream might have been more than nocturnal fantasy.

Meanwhile, in St. Elgos, the townspeople were shocked by the murder of Hart Northey, his body found in the stream where it had been dragged off the road. Two brothers named Hightwood were the primary suspects. Although a search of their home turned up clothing with telltale bloodstains, authorities were unable to locate the gun that had killed Hart. Even so, public sentiment ran so strongly against the Hightwoods that the two men were tried and sentenced to death.

George arrived in St. Eglos just before the Hightwoods's scheduled execution. Learning that his fears had been valid, the surviving brother was eager to avenge Hart's death. He went to the police and told them where they would find the murder weapon. The amazed investigators found the pistol exactly where George had said it would be. Asked how he knew its whereabouts, George replied, "I saw the foul deed committed in a dream."

MYSTICAL MASOCHISM IN THE SERVICE OF EVOLUTION

Stelio Arcadiou, who goes by the name of Stelarc, calls it obsolete body suspension, a sort of deprivation technique that symbolizes "the physical and psychological limitations of the body." The exercise involves placing eighteen large fishhooks through his skin, attaching them to wires, and then hanging from trees, cranes, or ceilings for as long as thirty minutes.

The suspensions, often performed before a spellbound audience, vary in design and intensity. Once Stelarc hung from the ceiling of a small, quiet room, surrounded by a circle of suspended stones. He described the session as being "meditative and peaceful," in contrast to the "noisy and disruptive" experience he had while dangling over a New York City street. And when he hung from a crane, 180 feet above the streets of Denmark, he admitted to being frightened.

But the exercises, he says, are necessary. "Technology has surpassed our evolutionary capability," Stelarc explains. "The body cannot cope with the quality or quantity of information that confronts it. Man is in a kind of evolutionary crisis—the body is obsolete. The next step in human evolution will combine technology with the body. Suspensions represent one of these evolutionary paths."

For Stelarc and his audiences, the suspensions are a realization of the primordial desire to be suspended in space. He remains within the limits of gravitational forces, but the audience witnesses the symbolism of man overcoming the force of gravity.

Stelarc has never had any serious medical problems as a result of his meditative performances.

THE FATEFUL VISION OF MARK TWAIN

While once staying at his sister's home in St. Louis, Samuel Clemens (better known as Mark Twain) had a disturbing dream in which he saw his brother Henry lying in a metal coffin. On the body's chest was a bouquet of white flowers with a single red rose in its center. Twain's first thought on awaking was that Henry was indeed dead, but the feeling passed quickly, and he recounted the dream to his sister in the morning.

At that time, during the 1850s, Twain and his brother Henry worked on the riverboats that cruised the Mississippi River between St. Louis and New Orleans. And a few weeks after Twain's dream, the two men were returning to St. Louis on separate riverboats, when the boiler on one of the boats, the *Pennsylvania*, exploded, killing most of the passengers, including Henry Clemens.

While most of the victims were later buried in wooden coffins, local residents contributed enough money to purchase a metal casket for Henry. In fact, viewing the scene, Twain realized that every detail of the funeral matched those of his dream—except the floral bouquet. Then, as Twain stood beside his brother's body, a woman entered the parlor and placed an arrangement of white flowers on Henry's chest—and at the center of the bouquet was a single red rose.

DOLL DISEASE

The reproductions of antique dolls were perfect, except for the black speckles all over their faces. Unable to stem the appearance of the spots, the young girl who had made each one by hand was distressed. Thinking that her sweating hands were responsible, she went to the office of British physician Conrad Harris.

The doctor decided to perform a simple test. Before firing a doll's clay head in her kiln, he instructed his patient, she was to draw a cross on its forehead with her finger. She should then repeat the procedure with a second doll, but this time while wearing a rubber glove. Sure enough, the glove-touched doll displayed no spots.

Having determined that the girl was the source of the problem, Harris set out to learn what exactly in her perspiration caused the reaction in the dolls. Guessing that it was sulfides, his supposition was confirmed when a dietary analysis revealed that the girl regularly consumed large quantities of sulfide-rich garlic. And when she stopped eating garlic for a week, the spots didn't appear on the dolls.

Harris's discovery, of course, has wider implications for the antique doll reproduction industry: Craftspeople in Italy, Germany, and France—with traditionally garlic-rich foods—regularly lose 10 percent of their dolls to the black spot disease.

A DEATH WISH COME TRUE

While many people may have a preference for the way they die, few ever die as they wish. American revolutionary patriot James Otis, however, did. He had often remarked to friends and relatives that when he died he hoped it would be the result of being struck by lightning. On May 23, 1783, Otis was leaning against a doorpost of a house in Andover, Massachusetts, when a bolt of lightning struck the chimney, ripped through the frame of the house, and hit the doorpost, killing Otis instantly.

CHINESE SEA MONSTERS

Pausing on the banks of Wenbu Lake in a remote part of Tibet, a Chinese Communist Party official watched in horror as a dinosaurlike creature emerged from the water, attacking and then devouring the man's prize yak. Although the sighting by a reputable observer was reported on the country's evening news, it was not the first time such an unidentifiable beast was seen. While in the mountainous region of Manchuria known as Changbai, Chinese author Lei Jia twice witnessed a black, six-foot-long lake monster in 1980. The reptilelike beast, he said, had a long neck and an oval-shaped head. Three weather bureau officials, having also seen the serpent, confirmed Jia's report. When they shot at it, however, the lake monster disappeared.

At the crater lake in northeastern Jilin province, moreover, tourists as well as the staff of a nearby weather station saw a serpent with a ducklike beak traveling through the water, creating waves in its wake as if it were a motorboat.

THE CURSE OF ROUTE 55

The planned construction of a 4.2-mile highway through New Jersey's Deptford township was greeted with adamant protest from Carl Peirce, a Nanticoke Indian also known by the name of Wayandaga. At a press conference, Wayandaga publicly predicted that the Route 55 project would be doomed because its intended path would traverse an ancient Indian village and burial ground. The new highway, he argued, would desecrate the graves of the Paleo-Indians, who had inhabited the area eight thousand years ago. He told officials that if they proceeded with the road, his ancestors would exact revenge.

The highway's builders, of course, didn't heed Wayandaga's prediction and went ahead with the construction. Before long, disastrous, and even deadly occurrences began to plague the crew. One worker was killed by an asphalt roller, while another was seriously injured when he fell from a bridge. An inspector was inexplicably struck down by an aneurysm in the brain. Yet another workman suffered three heart attacks during the course of the construction. The worst event, however, involved a van, carrying five crewmen, that suddenly and mysteriously exploded.

According to Wayandaga, deaths and injuries will continue to plague the project until the construction of Route 55 is halted or its path is diverted around the sacred ground.

MUTANT SPONGES

Some twenty-five years ago, 47,500 barrels of radioactive waste was dumped in the Pacific Ocean, just beyond San Francisco's Golden Gate Bridge. Today, the plutonium content of the seabed is twenty-five times what the experts originally predicted. Even more astounding is oceanographers' discovery, in the same area, of a new genus of sponge, mutants three to four feet tall, and shaped like vases.

THE TREASURES OF COCOS

If anyone ever manages to unearth the treasure of Cocos Island, the site of two separate nineteenth-century illicit deposits of riches, he'd be fabulously wealthy.

In 1820, the pirate Benito Bonito captured a Spanish galleon transporting 150 tons of gold and buried the booty on Cocos, an inhospitable Pacific island two hundred miles off the coast of Costa Rica. To maintain its secret location, he killed most of his crew and then sailed away. But he never returned.

Some years later, a revolution in Peru threatened the safety of invaluable state and church treasures, which authorities shipped to Panama. The captain of the *Mary Deare*, the vessel carrying the treasures, inexplicably altered his course and headed toward Cocos. It was the last anyone saw of the captain, crew, or the Peruvian treasures.

THE MYSTERIOUS MONK

Portrait painter Joseph Aigner was often despondent and suicidal despite his admirable talent and success. He had made his first suicide attempt when he was eighteen years old, but as he hung from the rafters of his family's Viennese home, he was unexpectedly visited by a Capuchin monk who somehow convinced him that life was worth living. Four years after that event, however, Aigner tried once more to kill himself, and again the same monk mysteriously appeared out of nowhere to prevent the suicide.

During the next eight years, Aigner became a revolutionary rebel and was eventually arrested and sentenced to death. Before the execution, however, he was reprieved—through the intervention of the very same Capuchin monk who had twice prevented Aigner's suicide.

In 1886, however, the sixty-eight-year-old artist finally fulfilled his death wish by shooting a bullet through his head. The funeral service was conducted, oddly enough, by none other than the Capuchin monk whose name Aigner never learned but who had successfully kept Aigner alive for sixty-eight years.

Vision of a Pope's Death

A member of Renaissance Italy's Borgia family, Pope Alexander VI was a master of depravity whose reign in the Vatican was rife with murder, incest, and greed. Alexander VI died in 1503, ostensibly from malaria, at the age of seventy-three. But according to legend, his death was overshadowed by more sinister and supernatural forces.

Before his death, Alexander VI had passed an edict declaring that the estates of all deceased cardinals would become the property of the Holy See. Then, intending to murder a particular wealthy cardinal with a gift of poisoned wine, the pope invited himself to the cardinal's home. En route, however, he realized he'd forgotten an amulet purported to ward off the effects of the poison. He would need it to drink the wine himself and not cause suspicion. So he sent a traveling companion, Cardinal Caraffa, back to fetch it.

Entering the pope's bedroom where the amulet was left, Caraffa was shocked to find a bier draped in black and lit by torches in the center of the room. Atop the bier was the corpse of the man for whom he was performing his errand—Pope Alexander VI.

Meanwhile, Alexander had arrived at the banquet where a mix-up in the wine goblets resulted in the pope drinking his own poison. A few days later, just as Caraffa had foreseen, the Borgia pope was dead and laid out in his bedroom, on a bier draped in black.

A Fiery Death at Sea

When Mary Carpenter, her husband, and children took off on their cabin cruiser for a vacation off the coast of Norfolk, England, they never imagined the tragedy that would befall them. They had been enjoying the weather on July 29, 1938, sunbathing on the boat's deck when Mary was suddenly and inexplicably engulfed in flames. As her horrified family looked on helplessly, she was reduced to ashes in a matter of minutes. Yet amazingly, nothing else on board was even touched by the fire.

The Language of Escape

During the Civil War, a small number of Swiss natives were soldiers in the Union army. When they were captured by southern Confederate soldiers, the Swiss Union soldiers were transported by train to a prison camp in Salisbury, North Carolina. Under the guard of a seventeen-year-old named Beverley Tucker, the prisoners planned their escape, speaking in their native language to avoid detection.

When the train stopped at a station along the way to Salisbury, the prisoners made the break. But to their surprise, a Confederate regiment surrounded them, bayonets aimed. Unfortunately for the Swiss, Tucker spoke their language, having gone to school in the same region of Switzerland where the prisoners were born and raised.

POKER JUSTICE

Robert Fallon of Northumberland, England, was an avid poker player, world traveler, and notorious cheat. He met his end after winning $600 in a poker game at San Francisco's Belle Union saloon in 1858: his fellow gamblers accused him of foul play and shot and killed him on the spot. But since money obtained through cheating is considered unlucky, the callous cardplayers needed to fill Fallon's place before they could resume their game. So they pulled in the first available passerby, who happily accepted Fallon's winnings as his stake in the game.

Instead of losing as the murdering cardplayers had expected, the new player increased the $600 to $2,200 before the police arrived on the scene. The law officers ordered the stranger to turn over the original $600 so that the money could be rightfully given to Fallon's next of kin. That, however, would not be necessary. It turned out that the stranger was, in fact, Fallon's son and it had been seven years since he had last seen his roving, poker-playing father.

THE MYSTERY MISSILE OF LAKEWOOD, CALIFORNIA

More than thirty years after the end of World War II, a missile from that period somehow crashed into the backyard of a suburban home in Lakewood, California. The twenty-two-pound shell hurtled out of the sunny afternoon sky and plummeted onto Fred Simons's patio, smashing a layer of concrete and creating a four-foot crater before coming to rest.

The local bomb squad dug out the missile and declared it was a dud containing no explosives. And at first, the Federal Aviation Administration (FAA) investigators theorized that a prankster had dropped the missile from a plane flying in the flight path from Long Beach Airport over Lakewood. But they monitored the flight tapes to determine if any aircraft might have opened a door and thrown something out. If so, the investigators would have heard a screeching sound on the tape, but they didn't come up with any evidence.

The Los Angeles County Sheriff's Office also launched a fruitless probe. The only thing they were able to determine was that the missile was not fired from some kind of tube or a cannon.

Lacking any clues at all, both the FAA and the Sheriff's Office dropped all investigation of the mystery missile, admitting they have no idea where it came from and will probably never know what happened.

CHANNELED SURGERY

Born in 1918 in Brazil's Belo Horizonte district, José Pedro de Freitas, known simply as Arigo, was a farmer's son who rose quickly in the ranks of the ironworkers' union. At the age of twenty-five, he was elected president of the local, but following a strike to protest dangerous working conditions in the mines, he was fired and went on to manage a bar in nearby Congonhas de Campo.

During the election campaign of 1950, one of the candidates, Lucio Bittencourt, a staunch supporter of the ironworkers, went to Congonhas to meet with his constituents. While there, he met with Arigo and was so impressed by the man's impassioned speech on behalf of the ironworkers, he invited Arigo to continue their conversation at the Hotel Financial where Bittencourt was staying.

During the night, Bittencourt woke to find Arigo, eyes glazed over, standing over him and holding a razor. Speaking with an atypical German accent, Arigo said the stunned candidate required surgery, which Arigo was going to perform. Bittencourt was so shocked that he fainted. When he later regained consciousness, and found himself still very much alive, Bittencourt realized that he was covered with blood. He felt a soreness toward the back of his rib cage, where he was surprised to see a perfect, neat incision. Quickly dressing, he confronted Arigo, who had no recollection whatsoever of the experience.

Unknown to Arigo, Bittencourt had been suffering from lung cancer, but when he visited his doctor the following day, X rays indicated that the tumor, in fact, was gone. When Bittencourt explained what had transpired, his doctor was amazed—the procedure followed by Arigo was performed nowhere in Brazil and was generally unknown by local physicians.

It wasn't long before Arigo was besieged by sick people from all over the country seeking his miraculous medical attention. Close behind them, reporters and psychics arrived to determine the source of Arigo's powers. During the next six years, Arigo would treat as many as three hundred patients a day, even performing knifeless surgery, while seemingly in a trance, and have no recollection of the feats afterward.

According to the reluctant healer, he had been having nightmares and visions since he was a child. At first, they consisted of blinding light and a voice speaking in a language unknown to Arigo. As the episodes increased in frequency, so did their intensity, leaving Arigo with painful, lingering headaches. But they also became clearer. He was able to discern a brightly lighted operating room, where a short, stocky, balding man dressed in surgical garb addressed a group of colleagues—in the same strange language that Arigo had been hearing all along. Eventually, the physician revealed his identity and his purpose: he was Dr. Adolpho Fritz, he told Arigo, and he had chosen the Brazilian to carry out his healing plan because of his compassionate nature.

Arigo would begin each of his treatments by saying the Lord's Prayer, during which he would go into another state of consciousness, which he described as "a state I do not understand." While in the trance, he'd perform surgery and write prescriptions, and he achieved a phenomenal success.

Aware that the medical community as well as the Catholic Church were disturbed by the channeled surgery, a local priest advised Arigo to cease his practice. But Arigo refused, insisting that he was merely the intermediary between the people and the spirit of Dr. Fritz. Then, in 1956, Arigo was charged with practicing "illegal medicine."

The trial was widely publicized, and the popular opinion of Arigo's work was overwhelming. Professor J. Herculano wrote in a Brazilian newspaper that it was "simply ridiculous to deny that the phenomenon of Arigo exists. Medical specialists, famous journalists, intellectuals, prominent statesmen have all witnessed the phenomenon at Congonhas. We cannot possibly deny the reality of his feats." Despite the support, however, Arigo was sentenced to jail, but granted probation on the condition that he give up his practice.

Sometime later, Arigo covertly resumed his mystical surgery, an easy task since local authorities tended to look the other way where Arigo was concerned.

THE ABANDONMENT OF THE MARY CELESTE

Navigating the waters east of the Azores on December 1872, the crew of the *Dei Gratia* sighted a brigantine bobbing on the ocean at half-sail. Moving in closer to investigate, they identified it as the *Mary Celeste*, whose captain was a close friend of the *Dei Gratia*'s captain, David Morehouse. The ship was deserted, having been hastily abandoned. Its captain, Benjamin Briggs, his wife, Sarah, his two-year-old daughter, and the crew were gone, although the cargo appeared to be in order. Ever since the *Mary Celeste* was found, the case has been mired in legend and rumor because no one has ever been able to determine what actually happened.

The captain's last notes, written on a slate but not yet entered in the logbook, indicated that on November 25, the vessel had been 370 miles west of where it was found.

There was nothing in the logbook that might have shed light on the fate of the Briggs family and the crew.

The attorney general of Gibraltar initially proposed that the crew had broken into the ship's barrels of commercial alcohol, gotten drunk, killed the Briggs family, and then escaped in the lifeboat. But that was improbable because the ship's alcohol would have killed anyone who drank it. Others, however, suggested that the captain had detected a leak in the flammable cargo and quickly abandoned ship. Or Briggs may have possibly ordered the abandonment because of a waterspout: a phenomenon that causes a change in atmospheric pressure that can blow open hatch covers and force bilge water up into the ship, resulting in the ship sinking.

What happened to the passengers and crew of the *Mary Celeste* remains a nautical mystery.

NIGHT TERROR DEFENSE

A 1987 murder trial in Great Britain revolved around a strange homicide with an even more bizarre defense. According to the defendant, he had dreamed that he was being pursued by Japanese soldiers and, in self-defense, he strangled one of his attackers. When he woke up, he realized that in his sleep he had strangled his wife instead.

Expert testimony during the trial attested to the man's suffering from a rare sleep disorder known as night terrors. Unlike sleepwalking, the condition involves intense emotional disturbances that typically include sensations of falling or being attacked. The afflicted often have realistic dreams in which they physically act out what is happening in the sleeping state—as the defendant had—and they remember little or nothing when they awaken.

A similar case was reported by psychiatrist Ernest Hartmann in his book *The Nightmare: The Psychology and Biology of Terrifying Dreams*. A Massachusetts driver, under the influence of alcohol, pulled over to the side of the road to sleep off his drunkenness. While asleep, however, he started up the car's engine, turned the car around, and continued down the road in the wrong direction, subsequently killing three people. The man was later convicted, but only because of the alcohol content in his blood. Under Massachusetts law, the driver was able to plead insanity because he didn't know what he was doing and could not, therefore, distinguish between right and wrong.

Psychiatrists in the British case, however, argued that the night-terror defense shouldn't enable someone to get away with murder, as happened in the case of the man who murdered his wife. Most other violent acts, they say, carried out in an organic confusional state carry a sentence of mandatory referral to a hospital.

BEWARE THE TWENTY-FIRST DAY

For most of his life, Louis XVI of France would not perform any important business on the twenty-first of every month, all because an astrologer had warned him as a child to be wary of the date. But it wasn't always possible for the king to avoid events he couldn't control. On June 21, 1791, Louis and his queen, Marie Antoinette, were arrested while attempting to escape the country during the French Revolution. The following year, on September 21, the institution of royalty was abolished in France and on January 21, 1793, Louis was executed.

THE DISCOVERY OF "NONEXISTENT" ANIMALS

Sir Harry Johnston first heard stories about the okapi from a group of Congolese Pygmies around the turn of the century. In 1901, he sent a whole skin, two skulls, and a detailed description of the mule-sized animal with zebra stripes to London, where it was determined that the okapi was a close relative of the giraffe. In 1919, the first live okapi were taken out of the Congo and placed in European zoos.

As early as 1812, paleontologists and other scientists were proclaiming that there was little likelihood of discovering new species of animals. But even then, with the discovery of the tropical America tapir in 1819, the fatalists were obviously wrong. Since that time, from the tapir find up to and beyond the okapi, there's been a string of new animals found around the world.

In 1909, for example, German explorer Hans Schomburgk set out to find the giant black pig of Liberia. It took years, but finally he spotted it—big, black, and shiny, but obviously related to the hippopotamus and not the pig. He was unable to catch it, however, and was forced to return home to face his skeptical critics. But Schomburgk knew what he had seen and, in 1912, returned to Africa in another effort to capture the animal. This time he returned home triumphantly with not one but five pygmy hippos, each weighing about four hundred pounds, one-tenth the weight of the average adult hippopotamus.

Many unknown or extinct species have been sighted on numerous occasions before one is caught and the physical evidence is presented to skeptics. No one, for example, believed reports about Indonesia's giant monitor lizard, said to be as long as twelve feet and weighing as much as 350 pounds. The stories about the monstrous dragon eating goats, pigs, and even attacking horses, were too incredible for skeptics to take seriously. Then skins and photos were offered as proof, and eventually a live Komodo dragon was caught and exhibited.

Other so-called nonexistent creatures included the mountain nyala of southern Ethiopia, the Andean wolf, and the kouprey of Southeast Asia. Even more interesting have been the discovery of "extinct" specimens. The coelacanth, a huge, large-scaled, steel-blue fish that scientists insisted hadn't existed for sixty million years, was discovered off the coast of South Africa in 1938. And as recently as 1975, the long-nosed peccary, a relative of pigs, boars, and warhogs that supposedly died out two million years ago, was discovered in Paraguay.

Perhaps the most extraordinary appearance (or reappearance) of an animal concerns the catching in a modern reinforced net by a Japanese fishing boat of what the Japanese fishermen thought was a sea serpent—or sea dragon—in the Pacific in 1977. It died *after* it was captured and after it had put up a determined resistance. It was approximately 35 feet long and a photograph of it taken at the time of its capture indicated that it had all the attributes of a pleisiosaurus, supposedly extinct since the durarsic era. As its body started to decompose, the captain ordered it thrown overboard. Only the photograph of the body and a detailed sketch of the animal show the extraordinary resemblance to what science believes the pleisiosaurus looked like. A number have been seen in the world's oceans but the 1977 photograph seems to prove that some have survived their supposed extinction.

CLOSE ENCOUNTER OF THE AIRLINE KIND

Eastern Airlines captain C. S. Chiles and his co-pilot, J. B. Whitted, had expected a routine flight on July 23, 1948. They departed Houston bound for Boston on a clear, moonlit night. At 2:45 A.M., a few miles south of Montgomery, Alabama, Chiles noticed a red glow heading directly toward the DC-3 with alarming speed.

At first, he thought it was probably some sort of new military jet and assumed that the jet's pilot, seeing the DC-3's red and green warning signals, would veer clear. It soon became apparent, however, that such would not be the case and the Eastern flight crew felt the sweat bead on their brows as they watched the jet continue toward them. Faced with no other alternative, Chiles banked his craft sharply to the left. He and Whitted got a good view of the oncoming craft as it passed about a hundred feet off the DC-3's right wing.

What they had thought was a military jet was a cigar-shaped and wingless craft with rows of windows illuminated by a blinding white light. It went into a sudden steep climb and then, with a flash of orange flame from its rear, vanished into the sparse clouds.

The late UFO expert J. Allen Hynek believed what Chiles and Whitted saw was actually a meteor, a logical explanation except for an important point: Meteors don't change direction and head back out to space.

THE RI OF NEW GUINEA

Anthropologist Roy Wagner had been studying the highland natives of New Guinea for more than twenty years when, in the late seventies, he switched his attention to the Baroks on the island of New Ireland. Living among his subjects, Wagner soon heard an intriguing tale about a *ri*, a mythical entity, that had washed ashore decades earlier.

Fascinated, Wagner assumed the *ri*, recognizable by its human torso tapering off into the body and tail of a fish, was a member of the extensive bestiary featuring mythical creatures in their legends and beliefs. There continue to be reported sightings, however, and tribal members all insisted the *ri* truly existed.

Some natives told Wagner they had, on occasion, eaten the *ri* they had caught and relished the particularly tasty flesh. A young boy reported a *ri* procession through a freshwater stream on a moonlit night. One man claimed he had seen a female *ri* caught in a fishing net. Still another had captured one of the marine creatures, but by the time he arrived back at the beach with Wagner in tow, the slippery *ri* had apparently escaped.

Curious about Wagner's account of the *ri*, published after his return to the University of Virginia, cryptozoological researcher J. Richard Greenwell decided to investigate the stories firsthand. And accompanied by Wagner and two geographers, Greenwell arrived in New Ireland in 1983. It wasn't until they journeyed to an area inhabited by the Susurunga, another New Ireland tribe, that the expedition team finally saw the *ri*.

One morning just before dawn, the *ri* searchers observed

a marine animal cavorting in Nokon Bay. It had a dark, sleek, slender body. It had no dorsal fin, but neither did it appear to have a human head or arms. Greenwell even managed to photograph the tail flukes as the beast dove below the surface.

Greenwell subsequently consulted numerous marine biologists, and has discounted the possibility that the offshore being was a porpoise or a seal. At one point, he thought it might have been a dugong, a marine mammal commonly found in the coastal waters around Australia and New Guinea. The creature he observed off New Ireland, however, traveled at great speed, unlike the slow dugong. "Dugongs, moreover, don't generally stay submerged for more than about a minute," Greenwell adds. "Our animal stayed down for ten minutes."

DEADLY CLOUD

According to a group of French astronomers, a giant, dense, interstellar cloud is on a direct course toward earth and it could have drastic effects on the planet's climate. Sometime during the next ten thousand years, says Alfred Vidal-Madjar, the cloud could block the sun's rays and, as a result, cause a new ice age. Alternatively, adds the head of research at France's Laboratory for Stellar and Planetary Physics, the sun could become more luminous.

Interstellar clouds are generally an astronomical mystery, but the French group speculates that the cloud approaching earth is somewhat cigar-shaped and roughly ten times longer than it is wide. Estimating the cloud's rate of travel to be about fifteen to twenty kilometers per second, Vidal-Madjar believes the cloud could already be as close as one-tenth of a light-year away. A precise prediction is impossible but, Vidal-Madjar points out, there's a remote chance that the cloud could start displaying its devastating effects as early as the year 2001, coincidently the common date foretold in a number of religions and legends in Europe, Asia, and the Americas, for the end of the world.

PREHISTORIC ATOMIC WARFARE

During the first part of World War I native officers of the British Indian Army often told their English counterparts that many of the so-called modern weapons were known and used in ancient India. These claims were accepted by the British officers with amused tolerance accompanied by the belief that these assertions were impossible and ridiculous.

Nevertheless some of these "tall stories" also appeared in historical accounts by non-Indian authors. Alexander the Great received an unaccustomed setback in a war against Porus, an Indian rajah who, according to Greek records, used explosive bombs launched by special artillery troops. The Greeks (and especially their horses), were considerably affected by this phenomenon, occurring as it did more than twenty-two hundred years before combat explosives were "officially" invented.

Ancient Indian books such as the *Mahabharata* and the *Ramayana*, both thousands of years old, include detailed descriptions of mercury-powered aircraft, projectiles that spread poisoned air in the enemy ranks and explosive rockets that followed moving human targets (like the sensitized rockets of today) even if they had to follow them "through the three worlds." In addition, a super bomb was used to wipe out enemy armies. It was called the "Iron Thunderbolt," incredibly described as being approximately the same size as a "Little Boy," which was the name of the first atomic bomb used in modern combat. The Iron Thunderbolt caused, when it was exploded, great clouds to form in the sky, which were likened to gigantic opening parasols, as compared to our own description of mushroom clouds.

The *Mahabharata*, not translated into English until the middle of the nineteenth century, was long considered by western readers to be solely an interesting religious and literary work. It was not until A.D. 1945, at the White Sands Proving Ground in New Mexico, that the *Mahabharata* was quoted in a scientific context by a famous scientist.

When the first atomic blast took place, J. Robert Oppenheimer, at the very time the mushroom cloud was ascending, used a quotation from the *Mahabharata* to describe his feelings:

If the radiance of a thousand suns
Were to burst at once in the sky,
That would be like the splendor of the Mighty One

. . . .

I am become Death—the destroyer of worlds.

The *Mausala Parva*, a section of the *Mahabharata*, has more to say about the effects of the Iron Thunderbolt, peculiarly reminiscent of the effect of nuclear bombs:

. . . it was a single projectile charged
with all the power of the Universe.
An incandescent column of smoke and flame,
as bright as ten thousand suns,
rose in all its splendor . . .
. . . it was an unknown weapon, an iron thunderbolt,

a gigantic messenger of death
which reduced to ashes the entire race
of the Vrishnis and the Andhakas.
. . . The corpses were so burned
as to be unrecognizable
Their hair and nails fell out—
Pottery broke without apparent cause
and the birds turned white.
After a few hours, all foodstuffs were infected.
To escape from this fire,
the soldiers threw themselves in streams
to wash themselves and all their equipment.

Were these strange parallels to our own experience merely an example of ancient "science fiction" or were they accounts of real events that destroyed a civilization thousands of years before our own developed?

ABOUT THE AUTHOR

Charles Berlitz was born in New York City. He is a graduate of Yale University and a grandson of Maximillian Berlitz, founder of the Berlitz Language Schools. He speaks twenty-five languages with varying degrees of fluency and is considered one of the fifteen most eminent linguists in the world. Mr. Berlitz was awarded the Dag Hammarskjold International Prize for Nonfiction. He lives in Florida.